SOMEBODY ELSE'S WAR

FRONTLINE REPORTS FROM THE BALKAN WARS 1991-92

Paul Harris

Only the actions of the just
Smell sweet and blossom in the dust

James Shirley

Spa Books

Produced by Frontline Publications for
Spa Books

First published in the United Kingdom 1992 by
Spa Books
P. O. Box 47
Stevenage
Hertfordshire

ISBN 0-907590-43-8   Hardback
ISBN 0-907590-42-X   Paperback

Published in the Republic of Slovenia by Gorenjski tisk

Printed in the Republic of Slovenia by Gorenjski tisk, Kranj

CONTENTS

List of Illustrations 6

Acknowledgements 11

Introduction 12

1 Baptism of fire 13

2 On the sunny side of the Alps 46

3 The highway to hell 62

4 The bridge at Pokupsko 70

5 Not so quiet on the eastern front 77

6 War on the innocents 89

7 Killing the messenger 95

8 Bosnian tinderbox 102

9 Return from Vukovar 121

10 All tanked up at the front 124

11 Don't they know it's Christmas? 130

12 Blue Helmets 138

Appendix I Chronology 143

Appendix II A note on the Strategy of the War 149

Appendix III *Dramatis Personae* 152

Appendix IV Notes & Bibliography 154

Abbreviations 160

Index 161

MAPS

The Yugoslav Federation May 1991 **48–9**

The Slovenian War **61**

The Republic of Croatia March 1 1992 **76**

Bosnia Herzegovina March 1 1992 **120**

ILLUSTRATIONS

Photographs by Paul Harris

taken between June 27 1991 and June 30 1992

1 The flag of a newly independent Slovenia is placed in the hand of the statue of France Preseren in the centre of Ljubljana, June 1991.

2 Burned out buses near Brnik Airport, morning of June 28.

3 "Take a look at the first bullet fired in the Third World War." The medical superintendent at Brnik Airport, June 28.

4 The roadblocks go up on the main Zagreb to Ljubljana highway early on the morning of June 27.

5 Buses are used to block the streets of Ljubljana, June 27.

6 Buses destroyed by tank attack.

7 Private cars still smoking in the car park at Brnik.

8 Hangar and Airbus A-230 of Adria Airways hit in aerial attack on the morning of June 28.

9 Damage inside the Adria hangar at Brnik.

10 Photographers working under fire, Turanj.

6

11 A January funeral for British photographer Paul Jenks, at Caythorpe, Lincolnshire.

12 The frontline at Turanj, Christmas Day 1991. WTN cameraman Zivko Krsticevic died here five days later.

13 Majda and Bojan Glavasevic in Zagreb, December 26. Husband and father Sinisa was kidnapped by Serbian troops from the Vukovar Hospital convoy on November 19 and was never seen again.

14 Going through the lines on the outskirts of Pakrac, September.

15 Devastation, Prekopakrac.

16 Defended flatblock, Pakrac.

17 VBR 128mm. rocket battery (type M-73), eastern Croatia.

18 The main Zagreb to Belgrade motorway at Novska. In happier times one of Europe's busiest motorways - the main link to Greece, Turkey and beyond. By September, Novska was the end of the line and only stray cattle used the motorway.

19 Saturday afternoon in September at the cafe, Jasenovac.

20 War trophy of dubious provenance. A Croatian soldier displays a Serbian Orthodox cross, Bosanski Brod, April.

21 Local people besiege the Federal army barracks at Samobor, September.

22 Resignation. Soldiers and police guard a bridge near Dubica, September.

23 Croatian guardsman, Jasenovac.

24 This M-84 JNA tank was destroyed by 'friendly fire' in the bitterly fought over front line village of Nustar, just a few kilometres down the road from Vukovar.

25 A T-55 tank joins the battle for the Bosnian town of Modrica, May.

26 T-55 tank, Turanj.

27 Early days of the war. A homemade tank based on a Second War James truck, Dubica.

28 Captured Federal army 128mm. Oganj rocket battery near Pokupsko.

29 TAM armoured police vehicle in the centre of Ljubljana, June 1991.

30 This woman seeks her missing husband at a prisoner reception centre in Zagreb.

31 Waiting for news of missing relatives, Zagreb, January.

32 The agony of waiting for news of relatives.

33 No news for this woman.

34 Lists of released prisoners of war are read out at the reception centre in Zagreb.

35 This man has just heard that his prisoner of war son has been released and is inside the centre.

36 Child refugees on the bridge at Pokupsko, September.

37 Young boy outside the presidential palace, Zagreb, August.

38 Bosnians flee by boat across the Sava, April.

39 Uncertain future. A young girl arrives by boat at Babena Greda, Croatia.

40 Refugees under fire flee across the bridge at Pokupsko.

41 For these young people the Yugoslav Federal Army is just a memory. Slovene youths celebrate in their old army uniforms in the streets of Ljubljana, March.

42 These young men have fled from Bosnia across the Sava at Babena Greda and are intercepted by Croatian soldiers: all men between 18 and 60 were returned to Bosnia for military service in the war.

43 Optimism in besieged Bosanski Brod.

44 Croatian military police dog unit, Djakovo, March.

45 Six year-old Budimir Mariocenevic at Ivan Dvor Lippizaner stud farm.

46 Lippizaner horses at the Ivan Dvor stud farm, near Djakovo, eastern Croatia.

47 Sixty year-old Rozika Militic, grandmother and tank commander *extraordinaire* from the village of Kamenica.

48 Snjezana ('Snow White') Paradzikovic from Semeljci in eastern Croatia. She joined the Croatian National Guard when the Serbs shelled her village.

49 After almost a year of war, crops rot in the fields near Vinkovci, May.

50 "Everything is gone." Peasant woman at Plostice, on the road to Pakrac.

51 Shattered ambulance, Vidusevac, September.

52 Mortar impact on the front of the church, Vidusevac.

53 Mass grave of Croatian volunteers who died fighting for Dubica at Tazan Church, September.

54 House destroyed by a direct artillery hit in the old town of Karlovac, Christmas Eve.

55 'Ceasefire' damage at Zagrebacki Blok, Vinkovci, March.

56 The church at Toran.

57 Blasted Baroque. Direct artillery hit in the centre of Osijek.

58 Repairing the damage of war at Vinkovci, May.

59 Roses at the gate. A home destroyed in aerial attack, Odzak, northern Bosnia.

60 The bridge at Zupanja blown up to prevent JNA tanks crossing into Croatia.

61 Shattered house, Turanj. The sad abandoned image of a young girl whose bedroom this once was.

62 On their return to Vinkovci, this couple find their home is beyond repair.

63 Impossible job? Clearing up at Nustar.

64 Humour in war. Police checkpoint, Bosanski Brod.

65 A UN jeep passes a destroyed house at Toran, near Pakrac in Sector West.

66 EC monitors at Turanj, Christmas Day. Eric Gautier (left).

67 Captain Ned Middleton of the Royal Army Pay Corps, attached to UNPROFOR, on his white-painted UN tricycle at sub-HQ Pleso.

68 Bagpipers of the Canadian contingent, November company, UNPROFOR Sector West, Sirac.

69 Outside the mortuary at Djakovo, Christmas week. The body of this woman's husband lies inside.

70 The grisly scene inside the mortuary.

71 Four year-old Alen from Valpovo refused to give up his life-size toy machine gun at the childrens' hospital in Zagreb.

72 This tragic nine year-old from Vinkovci had shrapnel fragments lodged in his brain.

73-4 Thirteen year-old Aleksander from Pakrac in the operating theatre at Zagreb's Institute for Mothers and Children. He was injured by shrapnel. The windows are taped over against air attack.

75 This boy flees from Bosnia at Gunja.

76 A Muslim girl flees from Bosnia across the bridge at Gunja.

77 House burning near Odzak, northern Bosnia, May.

78 A Serbian house destroyed by Croats in the countryside near to Bosanski Brod.

79 Burning house, Bosanski Brod.

ACKNOWLEDGEMENTS

Portions of this book have previously appeared in a somewhat different form in newspaper and magazine articles. I should like to thank the editors of *The Daily Express, The Times Educational Supplement, The Sunday Mail, The Scotsman*, the Dublin *Sunday Tribune* and *Scotland on Sunday* who have allowed me to use material from my features. Thank you also to WTN - and, especially, Sanya Mahac of the Zagreb Bureau - for giving me access to the English translation of Zivko Krsticevic's personal testimony of his work covering the war.

Many people have encouraged and helped me in this effort. Thank you to you all. But, especially, thanks to my travelling companions in the war zones: Igor, Cherry, Sherry, Judy, Mirjana, Alastair, John and Paul. We were lucky enough to come back in one piece. Then, of course, not forgetting Zivko, briefly known but not forgotten.

Paul Harris July 1992

INTRODUCTION

My guide in Karlovac, during a Christmas marked more by unremitting shelling and the sound of light machine gun fire than the conspicuous spirit of goodwill, was an irrepressible local English teacher, Mirjana Dosen. Ever cheery in manner and indomitable in spirit, she refused to allow the war which was literally on her own doorstep to interfere with life more than was absolutely necessary. In this she was like so many other civilians who had come to tolerate with extraordinary stoicism mortar, rocket and shell in the beleagured town.

She handed me a poem on Christmas Eve. I remember it rather well because as she handed me the poem, in the town centre orphanage occupied by refugees from the fighting, the sirens announcing an imminent attack sounded. The ever cheerful Mirjana was not going to allow herself to be phased by the sounds of the shelling around us. "Who do these Serbs think they are? They think they can frighten us with their big beards." Of course, it wasn't exactly their beards which were causing me a modicum of alarm. But, as I tucked into a handsome meal, in a now empty dining room, and Mirjana chattered unconcernedly on, I read and re-read the simple and moving poem. Even in translation it retained its elemental power.

Croatia, Autumn 1991

You are like the soil,
You are like the grass
Where tender flowers sleep.

Your wounds are terrible, deep:
The dead make you fertile,
The living remember you.

My farmers' houses are burning here
The childrens' dreams turned into nightmares.
And it is with fear that they expect the icy dawns.

Our hearts are burning for Vukovar, Osijek, Karlovac;
Dubrovnik, Sibenik make our souls ache.

Oh, my beloved country do not lose hope
Our spring is bound to come again
Grass will grow,
And tender flowers raise their heads.

Ljubica Koren-Zeljkova

12

1. BAPTISM OF FIRE

You wonder how you will react. You worry about how you will cope or otherwise. My own baptism of fire came in the besieged Croatian town of Pakrac. Very much at the sharp end of the front line, so to speak. I suppose it came as something of a surprise, that it was so easy to reach, and even pass through, a front line. It was also accompanied by an extraordinary sense of instant camaraderie with new found friends. It was both exciting and curiously uncharacterised by the sort of sheer, undiluted terror I always imagined exposure to attack by sniper, machine gun and mortar would bring. But, most disturbingly, there was what veteran war correspondent Edward Behr has described as "an inexplicable exhilaration in moments of danger" [1]. Moments of mortal danger are apparently marked by conflicting, atavistic emotions. And, in their wake, comes a strange inspiring feeling of increased inner confidence. Perhaps this is what *Life* photographer Tim Page was referring to when he observed, "War has always been glamorous." Peter Gill of the *Daily Telegraph* shared these emotions. "I can't explain it but there is something fantastically exhilarating about being terrified out of your wits." [2]

When I turned in to the BBC the noisy tape I had let run during that afternoon's concentrated attack on the police headquarters in Pakrac, they complained bitterly about the editing job. The editing out of the expletives. Nevertheless, it made a dramatic broadcast - even in its sanitised state. I sometimes play it back to myself at home by way of an antidote to notions of the glamour of war: to remind myself just what it was really like. In retrospect you tend to forget.

The fear of fear itself is incomparably worse than the actuality. Like before your first visit to a mortuary or the night you agreed to go into the operating theatre early the next morning to write about and photograph the battered and broken bodies of

13

children brought from the front line. Your own fear is always far worse than the experience itself. Experiences like this tend tell you as much about yourself, perhaps, as about the desperate plight of others, no matter how accurately you try to analyse objectively and record what you see. There are personal insights which which quite suddenly arrest you; and ultimately change you, the observer.

At this stage, I might point out that I am not really a war correspondent: a reasonably experienced writer and journalist but I don't have any particular penchant for wars per se. Human experience comes in all sorts of neat and not so neat packages, in which war sits uncomfortably in the latter. I'm really what has been described not so flatteringly as a "war tourist". P J O'Rourke is studiedly self deprecating about this role in his book *Holidays in Hell*. The vastly experienced Martha Gellhorn accepted the mantle more gracefully during the Spanish Civil War: "I had no idea you could be what I became, an unscathed tourist of wars." For myself, I observe and note what I have seen precisely because it is there and once you become personally aware of what is happening it is difficult to ignore, to turn your back: the demanding imperative of *témoinage*. War does provide excellent copy and more than a little richness of experience not to be gained anywhere elsewhere. The great thing about being a writer, of course, is that your role legitimises the endlessly fascinating activity of sticking your nose into other people's affairs.

You're walking down the street. It's busy with traffic and people on the pavement but everything seems normal enough. All of a sudden there is a bang forty or fifty yards up the street. Your reaction is instinctive - you duck into a doorway crouching with hands over head. Almost as soon as you do so you curse yourself for being such a fool. You remind yourself that Croatia is 1500 miles away and a whole day back in time. But the mind and body is still attuned to the slightest threat: a backfiring car in a city centre street is enough to send you diving for cover.

In the very real danger of war the idlest of bodies and the most phlegmatic of minds suddenly becomes highly responsive.

14

Sudden noises, low flying aircraft and that explosive exhaust all provoke an instinctive, self-preservatory reaction. And that's just as a result of photographing and writing about a war, let alone fighting in it.

That having been said, the bitter and bloody war in Croatia has often been said to have taken a greater toll on journalists than any, worldwide, since 1945. By the end of December 1991 it had claimed the lives of 21 journalists with a further three missing, at least two of whom were officially presumed dead. Claims at that stage that it had taken more lives than the Vietnam war were not strictly true: that conflict claimed 45 war correspondents killed, with 18 listed as missing. But these figures were, of course, over an enormously longer period - from the early 1950s up to 1975. Yugoslavia hit almost half that total of a quarter of a century in just half a year. In that sense at least it had already proved itself to certainly be the most deadly of conflicts for the journalist.

It is a war prosecuted with a particularly mediaeval, tribal brand of ruthlessness and hatred whilst involving the indiscriminate use of devastating modern weapons of war: Mig jets, rocket propelled grenades, wire guided missiles, mortars, multiple rocket launchers and heavy duty artillery. This in itself is not, of course, the explanation for the heavy body count among those fighting with the pen rather than the sword.

Few wars are straightforward affairs. But this is a hellishly complicated and unpredictable mish-mash of warring parties. In Croatia, there was, during the first few months of the war, on the one side the Croatian National Guard, police and local volunteer forces, relatively lightly armed and equipped, slogging it out against local Serbian rebels fighting a guerilla war with similar weaponry.

These rebels - the Chetniks - were backed up by the Serbian dominated Federal army (JNA or JA) armed with some formidable long distance firepower in the form of tanks (T-55, T72 and the more modern M-84); 155mm. howitzers; multiple rocket launchers (VBR, Oganj and Orkan) and little used aircraft (including Mig 21s and Mig 29s). Local warlords, acting quite independently of any central control, rather like mediaeval robber barons, emerged on the Chetnik side. In Serb dominated areas, self-proclaimed autonomous regions appeared under the control of men like the hardline, ambitious, 'irredentist' dentist Milan Babic in Krajina, and the more moderate Goran Hadzic in eastern Croatia. Supplementing these organised forces, throughout the Croatian held countryside and in many of the towns, were hidden snipers working their deadly trade from hidden locations like haystacks and flatblocks. Imported volunteer paramilitary forces added their efforts to the conflict: groups like the rumoured 1,000-strong Serbian Tigers led by Zeljko Raznjatovic, known as Arkan, a one time ice cream parlour operator and latterly a leading light in the Belgrade underworld, well known to Interpol. Such groups acted decisively in Croatia in the ealy days of the war as independent 'shock troops', living from the land and profiting from looting. In the spring of '92, Arkan transferred his and his supporters' attentions to the volatile situation in Bosnia - taking Zvornik and Bijeljina - in a re-run of their intervention in eastern Croatia.

In response to an initial inability on the part of the ZNG to control the depredations of JA and Chetnik forces, powerful and well trained paramilitary groups of a radical and right wing persuasion emerged under the control of groups such as the Zagreb-based HOS, the military wing of the Croatian Party of Rights. Dressed in black and bearing names like The Wolves of Vukovar, The Black Legion or The Yellow Ants, these groups operated independently of the Croatian government and were supplemented by foreign mercenaries, soldiers of fortune and anybody who simply happened to have acquired the taste for dressing up in a rough and ready uniform and bearing a Kalashnikov. Some of these groups became semi-officially organised, like the International Brigade fighting on the eastern front. It became not just a matter of Your Country Needs You. It became a war in which anyone was welcome to join in.

At its peak in this anarchic situation war was going on daily in dozens of different locations. In the first months, local

16

commanders fought their own private wars making reports back to HQ when communications permitted or, quite simply, when they felt so inclined. Unlike most wars, there was never a definable front line. It was quite impossible to tell when and where shelling, rocket or aerial attack would take place. Sometimes it would occur near to where forces were actively engaged but, as often as not, a decision would be made by some local commander to fire shells or rockets at a previously untouched civilian location up to 35 km. away from the action. In this situation survival became very much a matter of luck. Also, it was perilously easy to pass from Croatian held territory to that of the Chetniks, and vice versa. And neither side was accustomed to receiving visitors from the other side. Soldiers and policemen were decidedly twitchy. At first, most were quite untrained and inexperienced in the use and maintenance of the weapons they carried so nonchalantly. And large numbers were, quite simply, drunk much of the time. What has been called a slivovich war. Add to all this the hazards of mines sown apparently randomly by both sides with no location charts, unexploded shells and abandoned munitions, and you had an explosive cocktail which was inevitably going to take its random toll on large numbers of the participants, whether in uniform or otherwise.

But another factor directly affecting the press emerged early on in the conflict. Before they got an elementary grasp on public relations with the aid of Belgrade public relations consulting, just prior to the fall of Vukovar, the Serbian side in the conflict openly declared war on the journalists covering it. They believed that the Serbian cause was not being presented sympathetically enough to readers and viewers in the West. Their solution to the problem was unique in modern times. General Bidac Baubic in command of the attack on the eastern city of Osijek described the foreign press as "Croat agents" and, in the middle of September, set out to prove that he was to public relations what Genghis Khan had been to world peace. He attacked the Hotel Osijek, which then served as the press centre, with missiles. Fortuitously, most of the press were already in the basement but it was something of a miracle there were no deaths. It effectively constituted an open declaration of war which was confirmed the following week when he put out the order "Kill the journalists." First, that is. Before the military foe.

In areas where the Chetniks or the Serbian army operated, the use of press stickers or car markings became an invitation for trouble. Far from granting immunity, they only marked out such vehicles and their occupants for special attention. Some journalists seemed to have a surprisingly naive faith in their own immunity. Why this should be assumed I am not altogether sure. Immunity implies that both sides have some sort of interest in not impeding the activities of those claiming it: in the Croatian war it soon became quite clear that for many of the protagonists the reporting of their activities would actually have decidedly negative effects. Neither has the concept of immunity been aided by the fact that both sides in the fighting have used the supposed protection of Red Cross and press markings for less than altruistic purposes. It's also something of a moot point, as you approach the front with a couple of armed military escorts, whether or not you constitute a legitimate target. The Director General of the British Red Cross said in an interview in early December, shortly after returning from Croatia, that many Red Cross personnel had been fired upon deliberately and that he had felt more at risk in Croatia than in Iran amongst the Kurds.[3]

The outbreak of widespread fighting in Bosnia in April brought a degree of anarchy unknown even in Croatia. Newsmen and camera teams were, first of all, driven out of the Holiday Inn after Serbian snipers used the upper floors to fire on peace demonstrators below and shot dead six people. Journalists had their cameras and laptop computers stolen: tossed into their own suitcases or folded sheets and carried off by unknown gunmen. Some went to the Hotel Beograd which was attacked several times by trigger happy gangs. Other journalists then moved to the Hotel Bosna, on the outskirts of the city, together with EC observers and UN personnel. But it also soon became a battleground. A Visnews cameraman who boldly ventured out of the Hotel was shot in the arm. A WTN crew had their car and flak jackets stolen and were terrorised at a barricade by an unidentified group of men - whether Croats, Muslims, Serbian

18

irregulars, Bosnian territorials or imported fighters they had no way of knowing. Roadblocks, checkpoints and barricades most often were an excuse for acquisition of motor cars and the property of anyone with the temerity to venture onto the streets. Other cars were stolen overnight or valuable fuel siphoned off. Bosnia simply became bandit territory as the rule of law collapsed. Journalists were no longer the most obvious of targets: there were also plenty of EC observers and UN peacekeepers. A whole new variety of interesting targets.

All parties in the conflicts in Croatia and Bosnia have very effectively succeeded in dehumanising their opponents to a quite remarkable degree. The atavistic hatred of Croat for Serb, and vice versa, was quickly reawakened and exaggerated by local media. It was beholden upon the visiting observer to be aware of this at all times. Claims and counter claims of atrocities represented a metaphorical minefield as real for the journalist as its physical manifestation. A couple of days after the fall of Vukovar, Reuters news agency disseminated a story of the massacre of 41 schoolchildren by Croatian soldiers, as reported by a Serbian journalist. This was later completely discredited but the damage was done. Corrections were column fillers whereas the original story had made front page headlines and further fuelled the bitterness: significantly a day before the next round of 'peacetalks'. Reuters Belgrade subsequently issued a string of discredited press reports.

Until mid-October, journalists were granted virtually unhindered access to the frontlines by the Croatian forces. Initially, pressmen assumed that this was due to a positive eagerness on the part of the Croatians to have their story told to the world. In reality, it was probably due more to simple inexperience and general disorganisation. But then the Croatian attitude changed markedly: large tracts of the frontline were closed to journalists and the taking of photographs of military positions and, even, war damage became discouraged. On November 10, the Croatian authorities actually introduced censorship of some war reports. Shortly afterwards, it became common practice not to

19

identify in reports those parts of the front from which journalists - especially TV crews - were operating.

All this was only partly in an effort to cut down the death toll among journalists, although the Croatians became more sensitive to criticism after an incident on September 19 in the town of Petrinja. Local forces there allowed a French and a Swiss journalist to go walkabout on their own. Pierre Blanchet was a correspondent for *Nouvel Observateur* and Dominic Ruedin worked for Radio Suisse Romande. One of the duo stepped on a concealed mine and they both died.

Another incident pointed out the strategic dangers inherent in detailed war coverage when Croatian TV showed the aftermath of an attempted attack on a military headquarters. The camera obligingly panned from mortar crater to the undamaged building. Within minutes of transmission the Serbs had lobbed a mortar dead on target. It was, of course, precisely this sort of consideration which had led the British Ministry of Defence to deny news gatherers the use of electronic instant transmission facilities during the Falklands War of 1982.

Veteran American photographer Chris Morris, working for *Time Magazine*, was asked how he rated the risks in Yugoslavia. "I've worked in many difficult situations all over the world. If I'm asked to rate the dangers here out of 10, then I would give Yugoslavia 11."[4] The late Peter Jenkins, in *The Independent*, restated this view in a slightly different way, "Journalists who have seen action there think this is no good war to be killed in. It is the nastiest war they have known, vicious and indiscriminate . . ." [5].

Of course, the fact that a war is indiscriminate, vicious and nasty does not affect one's assesment of the basic issues of that conflict or, indeed, the necessity to be there. Ultimately, there surely can be no good war to be killed in - journalist or otherwise. But, if you have to go, it is better to perish in a conflict in which you can perceive some issue of right or wrong. And, to my mind, there has never been much doubt about the issues of right and wrong in Croatia or Bosnia.

Many journalists - too many - have died since the outbreak of the war in Yugoslavia in June 1991. The first journalists to die were two Austrians whose paramilitary-style jeep was hit by a tank missile, during the 10-day Slovenian war, at Ljubljana's Brnik Airport on June 28. In this instance, I am afraid to say, Nick Vogel and Norbert Werner must he held to bear much of the responsibility for their own demise. Their camouflaged jeep with wire grilles over the windows had all the appearance of a military vehicle: I know because my first reaction when I saw it that morning was to run for cover. Driving out onto the runway in full view of the JNA forces was at best foolhardy and at worst downright provocative: just about as provocative as the time Vogel exploded firecrackers in a crowd in Northern Ireland. He got great pictures. He also got put in jail and deported. Putting it bluntly, they asked for it. An Austrian girl who knew Vogel told me later that he had a death wish: if that was true then his wish was granted.

The vast majority of journalists exercise more care in where they go and how they conduct themselves when they get there. But there are no guarantees and there is a very large element of sheer luck involved. Vukovar was bad news for ITN's David Chater who was seriously wounded by sniper fire as he advanced into the centre of the city with Federal troops on November 15; also for Lauren van der Stock, an experienced French photographer with the Gamma agency, who was seriously injured there. Dubrovnik wasn't too lucky for *The Independent* reporter Phil Davison, who was hit in the leg by fire directed at the entrance to the Hotel Argentina, which he was sharing *inter alia* with the EC monitoring team. Fortuitously, his wound was not serious and the reverse evidently inspired a typically British stiff upper lip response. "A tourniquet from an International Red Cross doctor called Didier, a hip flask of Scotch from a young American journalist who helped drag me to cover, and I was later able to join with the ITN crew in an evening rendition of *Always look on the bright side of life*. The locals think we are nuts." [6]

On January 17 1992, British freelance photographer Paul Jenks died just outside Osijek. He had been in Croatia since the beginning of the war. *Daily Telegraph* photographer, Phillip Hollis, quite simply observed, "He was keen to go to places where others were not so keen to go." Thirty-year-old Jenks had himself written in the *Daily Telegraph* that the independent freelance "is drawn to that part of the conflict likely to yield the most newsworthy pictures: the front-line"[4]. Jenks was allegedly shot in the neck by a Serbian sniper. The entry wound was in his neck; the exit wound in his forehead. This led to some speculation that he was shot from behind the lines, by ill-disciplined irregulars or mercenaries, although observers whose judgement I trust tend to deny this. Jenks had himself written in tragic prophecy, "The risks involved are not often commensurate with the rewards."[4] The circumstances of death in the anarchic situation of the battlefield tend, inevitably, to be unclear. There is no coroner's court in some corner of a foreign field. Some of those who were on the ground maintain that he was, effectively, executed. Who knows? For him there was a curious and unexplained final indignity: the dead photographer's passport was stolen from his body. Contrary to what one might logically think, it is absurdly difficult to repatriate a body without a passport, even though the last breath is long since spent.

The greatest loss of life in a single incident involving the press was on October 9 1991 when an entire TV crew from Belgrade were killed by a direct hit from a Croatian mortar on their car: four men died. It has been widely alleged that a degree of mystery attaches to the incident. But then such stories are rife in the confused and anarchic wartime situation. Some journalists have certainly been evilly and deliberately done away with. Nobody actually knows the fate of Soviet TV reporter Victor Nogin and his cameraman Gennady Kurenoi. They went from Belgrade to the front line in eastern Slavonia to cover the conflict on the Serbian side. They were in a car bearing diplomatic registration plates. They simply disappeared: nothing was ever heard of them, or their Mercedes, ever again after September 3. After three weeks, a Russian search committee concluded that they had been killed.

Similarly, on November 19, after the fall of Vukovar, Sinisa Glavasevic, a well known and respected Radio Vukovar reporter

22

who had been injured in the course of his work two weeks previously, was abducted by Yugoslav army soldiers from the hospital convoy about to leave the town. He has never been seen since. He left a wife to bear his disappearance with dignity and a young son yet to appreciate the true implications of the disappearance of a father.

You are constantly reminded of the dangers. At a checkpoint on the road to Vinkovci in October, a grim-looking policeman asked us if we had any guns with us. We protested that naturally we did not. The response was unexpected. "You must be mad - it's very dangerous around here."

No matter how dangerous it might be covering the war as a journalist, there is one thing that ultimately separates you from those directly involved; those whose war it really is. As a foreign photographer, writer or broadcaster you can dip in and out of the conflict. You are not obliged to stay: whether by pressures of home, family or, even, voluntary frontline military service. For people caught up in a war which developed with such awesome speed, there is no choice.

Despite the patent risks, hundreds of journalists, photographers, radio people and TV crews have been - presumably more or less voluntarily - registered at any one time at the International Press Centre in Zagreb's Intercontinental Hotel. There can hardly be a country in the world that has not sent its representatives to cover this war and, at its peak, in the last quarter of 1991, Zagreb was flooded by pressmen. Out of this, inevitably, came the pressure to get a new angle, a different story or that picture which says it all: the apocryphal picture that's worth a thousand words. It was equally certain that one was more likely to get that stunning picture or heartbreaking story in the front line, rather than in the bar at the Intercontinental or at a press conference.

Many broadcasting organisations set up semi-permanent bureaux in suites at the Intercontinental. WTN (Worldwide Television News) set up there on the ninth floor at the beginning of the conflict and stuck with it for six months until the end of January. The BBC pulled out at the beginning of 1992 as the ceasefire took hold; its facilities were taken over for a while by Visnews. CNN established an office and although it has flown its own crews in and out, it has, by and large, relied on local crews and feed from WTN and other suppliers.

Some of the WTN experiences reflected the reality of "a war being fought largely with World War Two weapons and Middle Ages' brutality", as bureau chief Eric Bremner wrote in the WTN January 1992 newsletter. In a war with no definable front line, the experience of cameraman Olivier Quemener and assistant Alan Bubalo illustrates the difficulties. They were captured less than an hour from Zagreb by Chetniks and Serbian irregulars a full 10km. short of the battle front. They were taken to regional headquarters, interrogated, held overnight and then permitted to try to return to their car. After 36km. of walking with an armed escort, they failed to get back across the lines. The trip home was a veritable oddyssey: a 12km. hike, a 40 km. ride in a Federal Army truck, a 140 km. night taxi ride from Banja Luka to the Bosnian capital of Sarajevo, a 400 km. flight from there to Graz in Austria and a 150km. drive in a hire car from there back to Zagreb. This experience serves as a particularly graphic illustration of the complexities of covering a war with no real frontline, scattered pockets of fighting and a paucity of military intelligence.

In another incident, WTN cameraman Ivan Stankovic was shot by a sniper while driving near Kostajnica. The car turned over and landed in a ditch where the crew were pinned down by fire for several hours before escaping. WTN have lost count of the number of hire cars written off chasing the action in this war. But the first tragic loss of life for WTN occurred on December 30 1991 when cameraman Zivko Krsticevic died in a mortar explosion near the bridge at the frontline village of Turanj outside Karlovac. He was filming at the time. The camera continued running beside him as he died.

The dangers of the frontline are brutally apparent. Of course, it's one helluva lot safer in the sandbagged sterility of the modern Intercontinental or the cosseted 19th century luxury of the nearby Esplanade Hotel. I suppose you shouldn't really blame those journalists who either elected to report the war from there - or who are ordered to do so by insurance premium-conscious editors. One Dutch journalist, covering the war for his country's most influential daily, was unembarrassed about affirming that he had not been anywhere near a front line in two months of covering the war. And, years ago, I stayed myself in that 'front line' room in the Esplanade - the one with the red and white curtains which has been known to pop up on the TV news.

The more expensive hotels in Zagreb were often virtually empty save for journalists. The lady at a Jugoslovenski Aerotransport counter in Berlin was quoted in *The Times* as saying, "Only journalists have any reason to go to my country now. Maybe we will become like Lebanon: a country with no visitors, only journalists."[7] Pity the fate of countries at war.

Downstairs in the gilt and marble opulence of the softly-lit bar at the Esplanade the piano player tinkles out *All the Girls I Ever Loved* and the war takes on a romantic sheen as the alcohol reaches those parts even the music cannot reach. The bar is empty save for a few journalists, a couple of *whores de combat* and a solitary soldier in battle fatigues, a snub-nosed machine gun balanced precariously on the empty stool next to him. Outside, up the street, in what used to be known as Republic Square, the open space is thronged with pretty and fashionably dressed girls promenading of an evening for the men who stand in admiring groups. In the summer and autumn, the pavement cafes are packed and the bars buzz with noisy *bonhommie*. You could even become subject to a suspension of belief: it is difficult to believe that within thirty kilometres or so of the bustling capital men were fighting with a primitive, savage ferocity; dying in the fields, forests and ditches. That's exactly why it is important to get out there: in the context of Vietnam, Peter Arnett urged, "It's important for a reporter to see for himself all those thousands of little battles . . . to stand off and take a long-range view has been proved erroneous time and again."

By the beginning of March 1992 virtually all the foreign press had disappeared from Croatia following the widespread observance of the January 3 ceasefire and editors' concern with fresher stories in the disintegrating CIS and, indeed, rising tensions in neighbouring Bosnia. The absence of journalists on the ground on the weekend of February 29 - March 1 meant that several possibly significant stories went completely unreported in the international press and, indeed, only merited the briefest of mentions in the Croatian media. On the night of February 28, an estimated 500 shells fell on Osijek and the following night some 200 fell on Vinkovci. The next morning the extensive damage which was visible in both towns gave the lie to these being mere ceasefire 'violations'; these were deliberate acts of all out war perpetrated with cynical barbarity and which sent a very real signal of the breakdown of the January 3 peace accord. As one old man in his cellar shelter observed to me, "Where are all the journalists now? Where were you last night?" Upstairs, the flats at Zagrebacki Blok were wrecked by rockets which had landed on the roof.

The very next morning, Vinkovci was shaken by the greatest explosion of the whole war when the headquarters of the Croatian opposition party - the Croatian Party of Rights (HSP) - and its military wing (HOS) were blown up. Not by overt enemy action but by dynamite charges laid in the arsenal. Party leader Dobroslav Paraga, taking coffee in the nearby Hotel Slavonija, was twenty minutes late for an appointment there when the whole building went up at 1050 a.m. This attempt on the life of the leader of the right wing Croatian opposition went unreported in any foreign newspaper and, even, failed to be included in the reports of the state news agency, HINA. The events of that weekend demonstrated to me, beyond a shadow of a doubt, the importance of the reporter on the ground; of CNN man Peter Arnett's imprecation to "get in close", on the ground to actually find out for yourself what is happening in the war situation itself.

A combination of absence of foreign journalists and censorship of the Croatian media meant that the rest of the world, not unreasonably, assumed that the conflict had ceased in Croatia. In October, President Tudjman had signed a decree restricting press freedom and the offices of Croatian newspapers like *Glas Slavonije* in Osijek and *Slobodna Dalmacija* in Split have been raided. In Zagreb, the columnist Tanja Torbarina has been threatened with legal action by the Croatian authorities for "insulting the President." The sensitive Tudjman even threatened legal proceedings against *The Guardian* newspaper in Britain in a naive move which only assured him of continued rotten coverage in that paper.

The pan-Yugoslav television station Yutel has been obstructed in its coverage in Croatia, Bosnia and Serbia. Yutel's editor-in-chief, Goran Milic, was obliged to leave his home in Sarajevo after the so-called "justice minister" of the self-proclaimed Serbian Republic of Bosnia Herzegovina accused him of "direct responsibility for committing genocide on the Serbian people".

Similarly, the head of Sarajevo TV, Nenad Pejic, had to go into hiding and then flee the city after being put on a death list and hunted by Serbian paramilitaries. Sarajevo TV's coverage had been noted for its impartiality and spirit of compromise, despite threats from all sides of the political spectrum. Between November 1991 and the following January both the Serbian SDS and Croatian HDZ had proposed the division of the station into three national stations. In the words of Pejic, "We knew such an agreement would be impossible - the idea was simply aimed at destroying Sarajevo TV because it was professional and common to all of us." He adds, somewhat bitterly, "But if you try to be professional in a war you will not have success with either side. You are a traitor to both."[8] From the beginning of April 1992 broadcasters effectively took up full time residence in the TV headquarters in order to sustain broadcasting operations. Broadcasters - and their facilities - became prime targets and western viewers were duly regaled with dramatic footage of direct shell hits on the main TV broadcasting tower on May 5. Meantime, Serbian forces had siezed seven of TV Sarajevo's nine regional transmitters: they were turned over to broadcasting Belgrade TV.

In Belgrade, a nationalist leader, Vojislav Seselj, read out a list of "traitors" on television: mostly Serbs working for Serbian radio and TV. They were all subsequently sacked. The Belgrade daily paper *Borba* had its printing works raided by armed men unhappy about critical coverage of attacks by Serbs on Sarajevo. In December 1991, 150 journalists on the main Hungarian language newspaper in Vojvodina, *Magyar Szo*, went on strike after the province's Serbian authorities installed a new editor who was not a journalist, could not speak Hungarian and who supported the Socialist Party of Serbia, which had been instrumental in stripping the region of its autonomous status.

Following the imposition of sanctions by the UN and withdrawal of ambassadors from Belgrade, prominent elements in the foreign media there became targets for threats and violent attack. At the beginning of June, a Kuwaiti reporter, Yasin Rawashdeh, had a tear gas grenade thrown through the window of his flat. On June 12 *The Times* correspondent, 67-year-old Dessa Trevisan, wa shot in the hand as she left her home for a meeting convened to complain about threats to the press. A few hours later a telephone message from the 'League of Veterans' stated bluntly and chillingly, "We promised you a bullet and now you have had it. The bullet was infected with Aids." Journalists were now rapidly becoming the scapegoats for Serbia's year of unsuccessfully prosecuted wars, economic collapse and international isolation. As Mrs Trevisan put it from a capital now noted for gangsterism and increasing anarchy, "Such mass hysteria has been whipped up against journalists here that any psychopaths can take it on themsleves to attack. There has been a deliberate campaign against Western journalists since the coming to power of President Milosevic. The entire Western press is now accused of being in the pay of the Vatican or the Germans."

Despite the prevailing atmosphere of persecution and recimination, some Serbian journalists were courageously critical of the regime of Milosevic. A notable example was Milos Vasic, a journalist with the weekly magazine *Vremje*. He exhibited considerable bravery in penning an article for *The*

Independent in May under the headline 'God save us from our leaders'. Unequivocally, he wrote, "The Serbian people have been tragically failed by all its leaders: the ruling party, the opposition, the church, the intellectuals. None has been able - or willing - to articulate people's needs in terms that befit 21st century Europe. God help us: we have been destroyed by the Great Emptiness."[9]

Pressure on journalists was also increasing in Croatia. Reporting of the war by Croatian televsion (HTV) was initially of a high standard: detailed reports broadcast prominently at the top of the news from a range of local studios and landline links. By the end of 1991, the presentational structure had been significantly altered. Largely propagandist political items now came at the top of the news: wordy comment from Paris, New York or London. Short battle reports received scant coverage further down the news, reflecting a clear policy of minimisation of alarm and despondency in the civilian population.

The view was quite different out there on the ground. In the, then, only periodically shelled industrial town of Karlovac in October, less than 30 miles away from the capital, a policeman at a roadblock observed bitterly, "In Zagreb they don't know what it's like down here." WTN cameraman Zivko Krsticeviv encountered the same phenomenon, "People on the front line often reproach us that people in Zagreb don't realise the disasters going on. Go to Karlovac, that's only 15 minutes fast drive, and you will see a real war going on. You cannot compare life in Zagreb and life in Karlovac . . . in Zagreb war is not present at all."

I've often reflected on that myself as I cowered in some doorway in a shattered street. Maybe the guys hanging on in the hotel for the Croatian Radio news (thrice daily in English) were doing it sensibly after all. But I always felt a sneaking sense of superiority when I get back to the sandbagged haven of the Intercontinental actually having *been* there. In their sneakers and sweat shirts they eye me up suspiciously in my mud-caked army boots and ex-Gulf War NATO flak jacket. Of course, you don't tell them a thing. Otherwise your own very real experiences are likely to end up on the wire that evening with some hotel-bound hack's name on it.

In the bar at the Intercontinental the market price for a roll of frontline film can be as high as $200. A friend of mine, John, flogged his exposed, undeveloped film to an American photographer who hadn't moved outside of Zagreb in the week he'd been there. Then when the summons to return home came there was a certain desperation to return with some physical evidence of having done something about the job in hand. Personally, I've either never had enough film to sell or have simply been unwilling to part with what could have cost me so dear. The irony is that as a freelance one would indubitably make more money selling film this way than by having a few reproductions here and there. But I think it's an essentially unsatisfactory transaction. Especially for a chap who is keen enough to insist on actually standing watch on the processors back home while they put his films through the machine.

Without wishing to appear boringly self-righteous, I have also abjured the type of set-up or faked photograph which all too often appears in print. Even Robert Capa's famous Spanish Civil War picture *Soldier at the moment of death* is now generally believed to have been faked and it is a recognised fact that Joe Rosenthal's photograph of US marines raising the flag in Iwo Jima in 1945 was re-staged for other photographers several days after the original shot. The concept that the camera never lies belongs to a more romantic sepia-tinted age. Today, soldiers who sometimes appear to have missed a calling to the stage, will all too willingly pose as if under attack, fire off precious ammunition and even obligingly occasion some modest damage - all for the benefit of the less than scrupulous photographer. This sort of thing can, literally, backfire. A TV reporter for, let's say, XYZ News stood up in the front line on the Croatian side to do a piece to camera on a quiet day. Thirty seconds in, the most enormous mortar barrage started. Unbeknown to him, a few hundred yards away the XYZ team covering things from the Federal side had just been bemoaning the fact that nothing was happening. The Federals obligingly put up a barrage for the benefit of the cameras - almost wiping out their crew on the other side.

30

Some journalists and TV crews have consistently covered the
the conflicts with courage and determination. The world's press
found itself - somewhat to its surprise - in large numbers in
Sarajevo in April as conflict broke out all around. The Hotel
Bosna, where many of the journalists were by then staying, was
itself at the centre of a hard fought battle and it was possible to
cover dramatic engagements through the shattered windows. A
month later, the situation in Sarajevo had deteriorated to such a
degree that not only had the EC observers, most of the UN
personnel and the International Red Cross left the city, but also
virtually all of the world's press and TV. Apart from the locals,
the only TV crew left was from the British based Sky News: a
cameraman, a sound recordist and alternating front men Dan
Damon and Aernout van Lynden. They brought some
outstanding exclusive reports and footage of the worst shelling
to hit Sarajevo, amidst conditions of great personal danger and
discomfort. On June 7, a clearly exhausted van Lynden
described their efforts to obtain water and food and observed
bitterly, "Most journalists seem to be stuck in Belgrade for one
reason or another." Their coverage became important but did
lead to the anomalous situation whereby Sky regularly showed
the seriousness of what was happening to Sarajevo whilst the
situation was some days left quite uncovered by BBC or ITV
who had no on the ground coverage.

For those pressmen actually out in the field it's a mixture of
Scouting for Boys and those family treasure hunts you used to
go on of a Sunday. It's amazing how quickly you re-learn
dormant, half-forgotten skills: reading a map, using a compass,
tying up a pair of boots, travelling without the encumbrance of
luggage. I take enough in the six pockets of a fisherman's
bodywarmer, worn over NATO combat body armour fashioned
from Kevlar artifical fibres, to last me up to four days. The
contents resemble those of an affluent and precocious schoolboy
with military and/or medical ambitions: Swiss army knife, book
of matches, hip flask of whisky, 10 spare films, labelled empty
film canisters, passport, press card, Croatian Ministry of
Information pass plus a local military pass if required, chocolate,
a large shot of brandy, aspirins, indigestion tablets, field
dressings, Savlon, Dextrosol, personal medication, lip chapstick,

miniature toothbrush and toothpaste, toothpicks, bar of soap, electric shaver, condoms, compass, photocopied and folded maps, binoculars, two cameras (in addition to the one round my neck), 200 mm. and wide angle lenses, spare batteries, spare pair of glasses, notebook, pens and pencils, credit cards, cash in five currencies [Croatian dinars, Yugoslav dinars, German marks, Austrian schillings and pounds sterling], woollen fisherman's gloves with open fingers, spare socks and underclothes. In fact, just about everything except a conker and a dead frog.

'Be Prepared' isn't such a bad motto. In this one, at least, I find myself in agreement with the eccentric but canny Lord Copper of *The Beast*. "There are two invaluable rules for a special correspondent - Travel Light and Be Prepared. Have nothing which in a case of emergency you cannot carry in your own hands." [9] It is indeed much the most sensible thing to be totally mobile and independent. Almost carefree. It's a good feeling in some ways. A feeling I'd almost forgotten. Until Croatia, the idea of going to bed with your boots on would have struck me as nothing more than a display of vulgar bad manners.

It was after midnight and my driver and I were exhausted - and lost. We had reckoned on getting some sort of hotel room in the once thriving industrial town of Karlovac. Every single hotel had put up the closed sign and the proprietors to a man and woman seemed to be hiding in basements and cellars. The best hotel - the Koruna - located on the riverfront in a once idyllic situation now quite simply faced directly onto the Serbian lines on the other side of the water. It was no longer a residential option. We headed out of town stopping at roadblocks and checkpoints.

After much exhibition of documents and constellations of flashlights shone into our faces we were directed to a motel on the outskirts of the village of Duga Resa. Even allowing for the blackout, the large modern building didn't appear to be a centre of the sort of activities you associate with jovial mine hosts awaiting the hungry, tired, even thirsty, traveller. A noisy

32

2 Burned out buses near Brnik Airport, morning of June 28.

Opposite page:

1 The flag of a newly independent Slovenia is placed in the hand of the statue of France Preseren in the centre of Ljubljana, June 1991.

4 The roadblocks go up on the main Zagreb to Ljubljana highway early on the morning of June 27.

3 "Take a look at the first bullet fired in the Third World War." The medical superintendent at Brnik Airport, June 28.

5 Buses are used to block the streets of Ljubljana, June 27.

6 Buses destroyed by tank attack.

7 Private cars still smoking in the car park at Brnik.

8 Hangar and Airbus A-230 of Adria Airways hit in aerial attack on the morning of June 28.

9 Damage inside the Adria hangar at Brnik.

10 Photographers working under fire, Turanj.

11 A January funeral for British photographer Paul Jenks, at Caythorpe, Lincolnshire.

12 The frontline at Turanj, Christmas Day 1991. WTN cameraman Zivko Krsticevic died here five days later.

13 Majda and Bojan Glavasevic in Zagreb, December 26. Husband and father Sinisa was kidnapped by Serbian troops from the Vukovar Hospital convoy on November 19 and was never seen again.

assault on the locked front door ultimately brought an aged retainer to life rubbing the sleep from his eyes. He was the only occupant: a security guard put in after the last guest had left the hotel more than two months previously. Could we stay? He shrugged his shoulders. Why not? Why not indeed. I wasn't going to make a point of my freelance work for the Egon Ronay Guide. He waved at a large wooden key board which must have had 100 keys on it. We took our pick.

Upstairs, let's just say it was more than a trifle chilly. The beds were so damp I could see it was going to be like sleeping in a cold compress. We didn't dare switch the lights on. Then the sound of heavy artillery fire started. At this point, I resolved to insert myself between the blankets exactly as I was - boots and all - pulled them over my head and consoled myself with the thought, "This is war, after all".

The roadblock or checkpoint is a fact of life in any country at war. You soon learn elementary roadblock technique after a few menacing Kalashnikovs have been levelled at you. As soon as you see the roadblock you start to slow down; you wind down the window and place the British passport in clear view on the dash; if your headlights are on you douse them and proceed on sidelights; when you come to a halt you switch off the engine and place both hands in full view on top of the wheel. It's better not to have a seatbelt to undo. You don't jump out of the car, point the 200mm. lens through the windscreen, or reach into your inside pocket for the passport. These can all be actions with unfortunate and dire results attaching.

I am happy to be able to report that the trusty old British passport still seems to command a curious and almost universal respect. I'm speaking about the old hardback variety - I don't know about the floppy plastic covered EC thing which is insidiously making its appearance these days. On one trip I mistakenly took my 15 year-old British passport instead of my current one. I wandered around Yugoslavia without challenge such is the inherent gravitas of the document. Absolutely nobody noticed until I presented myself back at immigration at Gatwick Airport.

It's vital to perfect the art of rapid rapport with policemen, soldiers and anybody else who seems to have some influence in the department which holds the power over life and death, i.e. anybody who carries a gun. The important point is that is far more difficult for one man to get round to killing another man who is evidently trying to make friends with him. Also, the notebook, pencil and camera are quite ineffective bits of equipment in an adversarial situation. Cigarettes (not kept in that inside pocket), chocolate, some words of local lingo and a ready smile are your best assets. Nylons are out of fashion. Anyway, they wouldn't have fitted most of the guys I've met.

All that having been said, I'm not averse to fending off with the back of my hand a carelessly pointed gun poked through the window of the car. These guys were never even in the army cadet force, let alone the real army. The barrels alternately trail in the mud, serve as improvised shooting sticks or are, quite simply, regarded as the ultimate *macho* symbol. The use of the safety catch would be positively cissy.

Possibly the most unpredictable type of checkpoint is what I term the "freelance" one. This is often a one man, determinedly local operation. Typically, it's on a Sunday morning and Josip, or whoever, has had a row with the wife. The prospect of all day at home is just too much to handle so he digs out - sometimes literally - that old Second War rifle or machine gun and sets himself up at the nearest crossroads. Every passing vehicle, except those of his neighbours who are probably off to terrorise some other neighbours, is stopped and rigorously checked. No matter there is not even a passing knowledge of documentation - let alone any foreign languages - you simply have to resign yourself to an extended pantomime performance.

The very nature of the war has made photographing it difficult. I've probably missed some of the best photo opportunities through sheer panic and a primitive, if pathetically irrational, desire for self-preservation. Professional photographers with more experience than me - albeit with weddings, car crashes and other aspects of the rich panorama of British life - tell me they would have been quite able to handle situations which defeated me. Maybe they would. But it's a tough one to change lenses on your sole surviving camera on a bridge packed with hundreds of refugees, horses and cattle, all of whom have been launched into one great stampede by a sudden artillery bombardment. I just ran with them. When that 155mm. - or was it 128mm.? - howitzer shell exploded in the road 100 yards ahead I raised a camera to catch the flash of the explosion and the rain of debris. In the event, the lens of the quick use autofocus camera was still firmly closed.

Equally, it's impossible to capture a hidden sniper with the camera shutter. And you don't have a clue where the next shell will land unless, like they did in Vinkovci, they're landing ahead and behind you and getting closer all the time ... Nevertheless, when you get back home you can bet your bottom dollar picture editors will subscribe to Robert Capa's dictum on war photography. "If your pictures aren't good enough, you're not close enough." You can, of course, uncharitably point out that Capa's untimely end came when he stepped on a landmine south of Hanoi in 1954. And Zivko, a Croatian cameraman I knew who worked for WTN, died in Turanj trying to get still more of those close up pictures. The demands of the job mean getting the pictures tends to be infinitely more dangerous than collecting the words.

Editors also tend only to publish war photographs which fit neatly within certain preconceived boundaries of 'taste'. They are not in the business of upsetting the reader over breakfast with disturbing images of death and injury. A soldier with some superficial wound or sporting a bloodsoaked bandage is eminently suitable breakfast reading fodder: not a chap with his legs blown off after stepping on a mine, or those pictures taken in the mortuary of soldiers tortured to death. Television programme editors share much the same views, as Michael Nicholson found: "They contrive a surrogate war, where much of the suffering is deleted. They help to sanitise war; they almost make it acceptable." [10]

The moment of decision for the TV news directors came in the last week of May 1992 when TV Sarajevo shot and made available the most explicit and shocking footage to date. During a ceasefire in the capital, a queue of people waiting for bread was mortared without warning by Serbian irregulars. The images of shattered bodies, the blood on the pavements, the limbless screaming for help would say more to the world than any footage previously shot. There was clearly a dilemna over whether or not to show the film. In its first reports, CNN ran the sound, without pictures, over a map of Bosnia. German and Austrian channels immediately broadcast the footage, as it did Sky TV. By later in the day minds were made up in the most anaethsetised of editing suites and the whole world was seeing all the horror and distress of Sarajevo. The result was that within 24 hours the UN was putting in hand sanctions against Serbia. That was the measure of the effect of those appalling images.

Aware that some of my own pictures will never be published, I have been forced to try to perfect the written words to convey to the reader what he will not see presented visually: like the scene at a mortuary or the horror of operations on battle wounded children. As John Taylor points out in *War Photography: Realism in the British Press (1991)*, "Usually, it is not the process of dying which is visible in the press, only the aftermath; and then much of the thrill lies in imagining the process."

Photographs and war reports can help to change the course of a conflict as those pictures of the Sarajevo bread massacre did, and, indeed, it must be every journalist's dream to write a story or take a picture which has such a dramatic effect. Alas, it is very rare: increasingly rare in a world where the televisual image is today so powerful. Yet, occasionally, a picture can awaken the conscience of a people. Just as the *Life* photographs of the My Lai massacre, or Eddie Adams' famous 1968 picture of South Vietnamese police chief Colonel Nguyen Ngoc Loan blowing out the brains of a bound Vietcong prisoner did with the conscience of America in the Vietnam war, there were a couple of important, if less obvious, turning points in the Croatian war: the dramatic images of the shelling of the historic city of Dubrovnik and the moving human images after the fall of Vukovar.

The shooting of the Vietcong prisoner found its uncanny parallel in pictures from the Bosnian town of Brcko widely published around May 9: a Serbian policeman was photographed shooting two Muslims accused of being snipers in the back of the head with a machine pistol fitted with a silencer. A few weeks previously, in nearby Bijeljina, photographers had recorded the execution of a Muslim family of four and the the death of a local journalist, thrown from the top floor of a police station.

The physical dangers in garnering the written and visual images of war are well documented. The psychological aspects less well so. That is altogether more personal. It's quite impossible to know how you will behave under fire until the situation develops. The not knowing - the pushing at the boundaries of your own experience - is, of course, all part of the experience; what gives the whole experience that edge and exhilaration. The great fear before the first experience is that you will simply panic: either be frozen into terror or turned on your heels. War photographer Don McCullin, who survived more than twenty years of photographing wars, once said in interview: "This was always my golden rule in war: never panic - I'd seen so many men who'd died because they were shot in the back running away from a battle."[11]

Careful choice of travelling companions is important. I don't necessarily subscribe to the axiom, "He travels fastest who travels alone." While it may be strictly true, people on their own are far more likely to disappear without trace than those in company. An essential requirement is a driver with a good knowledge of the Croatian language. Travelling on your own is dangerous. It's also invaluable to have someone with you to discuss the options and the dangers. What the Americans call the 'Buddy, buddy' principle. You then act on a consensus view of your joint position.

Instincts are also important. If you don't feel lucky when you wake up in the morning you're best not to venture out that day, in my view. If you have a bad feeling going up to the frontline then turn back. Do a hospital, a mortuary or a refugee camp instead. And if you don't feel good about your travelling companions, bail out. During the Slovenian War I joined a carload of Hungarian journalists who couldn't read maps, adorned the car with enormous press stickers and each one of whom had a different idea as to where we should go. At the first roadblock I got out and walked back to the hotel. On my foray to the beleagured town of Pakrac I travelled with two female, American journalists. This had an upside and a down side. We all got the benefit of Grade 1 protection from all the local Rambo types; but I had to stop half a dozen times for visits to the "bathroom".

Perhaps one of the few positive things about war is the way friendships are formed quickly. You're never alone in a war zone. Men you might never even speak to in normal times - or feel you could hold any common ground with - become friends very quickly. Women you might never have seen as partners can become lovers within hours. Living for the moment; a conviction brought about by a sense of impernanence; a sudden realisation of somewhat different priorities. Unless you are exceptionally insensitive or impervious to what is happening around you, you start to learn more about yourself than you have ever been conscious of before.

Most journalists are either wordsmiths or photographers. They are scribes or photojournalists, and I can well remember how, not so long ago, there was no meeting point for what was regarded as two very different skills. Doing both words and pictures is still unusual but for me it has provided a positive niche. As I work, I mentally weave words and pictures together. With a background in book and magazine publishing, I can usually see a feature in my own mind's eye with text and pictures laid out. When you get back, the features editor doesn't have to cast around for suitable photographs to illustrate your words. You have a complete package to offer.

The really important thing is to make notes constantly as things happen around you. Steinbeck hit the nail on the head when he averred that unless you "made notes on the spot you could not remember how you felt or the way things looked." Those notes are also invaluable for longer term use: in writing this I have

38

gone back time and again to pick up some forgotten detail from notes which were intentioned for more ephemeral newspaper publication and which never made it into the actual paper.

The lot of the freelance is not an easy one. As you pass the American Express card to a seemingly endless stream of airline booking clerks, hotel receptionists, hire car operators and head waiters, you know that, as sure as hell won't freeze over, the monthly account will pitch up in the post the next month with unerring regularity. Unlike the cheques in payment for your words and pictures. And, if you're really unlucky, the exchange rate applied to your transactions when they come home to roost will be 300% worse than the advertised local rate at the time.

Oh for the lot of Mr Henry Morton Stanley of the *New York Herald* who interrogated his editor about his expenses for an important overseas trip and was given this open handed response: "Draw a thousand pounds now and when you've gone through that draw another thousand; and when that is spent draw another thousand; and when you have finished that draw another thousand, and so on. But find Livingstone." In the end of the day he had gone through £9,000. But he had one of the stories of the century - and the security of mind, while he worked on it, that there was something approaching a bottomless pit in terms of resources.

Not so for the freelance, American Express cardholder, alas. And, unlike the staff man, if the worst does happen in the field and you stop a bullet or some shrapnel, odds are you won't be spirited away by Europ Assistance in a private jet or helicopter. Odds on, you'd have to sweat it out in a field hospital not so far from the front line. There seems to be a widespread myth the war correspondent belongs to some international highly paid elite. Nothing could be further from the truth. One national paper while has printed my Croatian photographs regularly pays just £26 a time for the privilege. I know of several staff photographers who have actually paid their own expenses to get to the front in Croatia so summoned by the challenge did they feel. And for some, what could have been a costly expedition proved fruitful in results that might never have emerged back home. Like colleague Paul Hackett of *Scotland on Sunday* who travelled with me over Christmas in Karlovac and Turanj. Within a couple of months, he had been awarded *The Observer* David Hodge Memorial Award for his photographs: a deserved but essentially rare bonus. The only British journalist I've ever run across actually in the frontline was a photographer from *The Times* - near Dubica - who had managed to get just a week in Croatia from his picture editor, with considerable difficulty. For that matter, I've never met anybody who would actually cover a war like that in Yugoslavia for the money. Don McCullin summed it up in his autobiography, " . . . danger money never came into it. And really, when you think about it, the idea is laughable. The amount of money that would compensate you adequately for getting your head blown off doesn't exist."[12]

On return to Britain you become only too well aware that Neville Chamberlain's dictum still holds good to an uncomfortable extent. "A quarrel in a faraway country between people of whom we know nothing." [13] What applied to Czechoslovakia in 1938 still, to a large extent, applies in the context of Yugoslavia today. Editors in Britain are aware that their readers have but a limited tolerance of sustained coverage of the war. As the aforementioned Lord Copper so succinctly put it, "The British public has no interest in a war which drags on indecisively." Indeed, the readers of the mass circulation *Sun* voted coverage of the Yugoslav conflict as the most boring subject up with which they had to put. Even those of more developed intellectual fibre, I have found, admit to a general lack of understanding and a considerable degree of resigned apathy. It is difficult to get passionate about a place you neither know no understand - no matter how much you may have enjoyed that holiday in Dubrovnik ten years ago.

But when you have lived it - when you have been there and experienced it - it is only too easy to become passionate. When you return to Britain it is difficult to come to terms with the fact that the newspapers and TV news are not as preoccupied as you are with telling the story of all that wanton, senseless death and destruction. It is equally easy to become partisan about this war. To see it in terms of bad guys versus good guys. The big

battalions of the Communist invader against the valiant
defenders of the homeland. I think these are natural reactions
and ones which a professional journalist has, as best he can, to
rationalise and by so doing avoid undue influence. It is difficult
to find any moral basis for the savagery inflicted by either side.
W H Auden's "Those to whom evil is done, do evil in return," is
just about the most sympathetic construction you can put on the
conflict.

Putting it all down on paper can be surprisingly difficult: it may
appear deceptively easy to express in words all that you may have
seen in a week at the front. Certainly, enough has probably
happened to fill a couple of notebooks. There is never any lack of
the dramatic and tragic in a war zone. A half-wit could work out
where there will be stories - try starting with a few front line
positions, hospitals, mortuaries and a civilian shelter or two.
"Nothing makes an easier lead sentence than a stray mortar
round hitting a starving baby in a typhus hospital"[14].

In fact, there is so much to write about that it is sometimes a
problem sifting and organising your material. A typical day - at
the beginning of Christmas week 1991 - started in Osijek with
shelling and machine gun fire audible from a hotel room with
no windows and no ceiling. Then there was the breakdown of
talks taking place between Croatian and Federal army generals
in the centre of the city. Lunchtime (notably without lunch) was
spent in a mortuary 25 km. or so away in Djakovo where the
bodies of Croatian National Guardsmen were just being brought
in: they had been particularly brutally killed. Then there was an
abortive attempt to get to the frontline with retreat under
shellfire. And a visit to a Lippizaner horse farm where three or
four million pounds worth of equine investment whinnied and
pawed the stable floor as the noise of advance drew ever nearer.
At the end of such a day you're not sure whether you have one
major feature or three or four smaller ones and only reflection
and, possibly, further experiences help to crystalise this
confusion.

I write on the 'plane on the way home with those notes at my
elbow. At that stage, the response is overwhelmingly emotional,

often chokingly so; and this has to be balanced with rationality and a cooler analysis. You have to remember to give the reader a balanced view which will enable him to reach his own conclusions no matter how strongly you feel yourself. This, I find, will take several hours - if not days - and these elements have to be sifted and sorted out by the imperfect and emotional computer that is the human mind. Should this difficulty be ascribed to a lack of professional detachment, I wonder? Is a more world weary, cynical view called for? For me that is not an option: not with that previous knowledge of a beautiful and once peaceful and successful country so suddenly and devastatingly torn apart.

"The first casualty when war comes is truth." Senator Hiram Johnson is credited with first uttering these oft repeated words as long ago as 1917. Whilst not seeking to change or distort the facts, there sits, nevertheless, a particular personal onus to tell the story as you see it, as you interpret it; and thus to communicate effectively what is happening. You cannot be completely objective and, in any case, I do not go with that sort of ruthless detachment. While it is clearly immoral and dishonest to mislead the reader by telling of that which did not happen, equally events can often be more effectively put over by glossing over the nuances, by running incidents together and by imputing a reaction or an attitude. So long as this can be justified in the context of a general accuracy then this would seem to constitute permissible journalistic licence. Inevitably, this is sometimes called in to play to cover up one's own inadequacy: an inability to express what one has seen and which in itself can produce a despair almost as black as those events themselves.

Jim Lucas of the US Scripps-Howard group was a more than averagely experienced combat correspondent when he ended up in Vietnam. He had eight battle stars, the Bronze Star and the Distinguished Service Award of the Marine Corps League. He could analyse this sort of situation. "You know it's war when you see a young man dead. Young men court danger as they court women, and for much the same reasons. . . secretly each wants to be a hero, in the finest and best sense of the word, and there's nothing wrong with that, because quiet heroism is the stuff of war."[15]

I envy the facility of journalists like J A MacGahan. His report from a Balkans massacre was indubitably one of the most effective pieces of reportage I have ever read. "There were little curly heads there in that festering mass, crushed down by heavy stones; little feet not as long as your finger on which the flesh was dried hard . . . little baby hands stretched out as if for help; babes that had died wondering at the bright gleam of sabres and red hands of the fierce-eyed men who wielded them; children who had died shrinking with fright and terror; young girls who had died weeping and sobbing and begging for mercy; mothers who died trying to shield their little ones with their own weak bodies, all lying there together . . ."[16].

That was actually written in 1876 but it could just as well have been written in the last decade of the 20th century. There were echoes of it in Ed Vulliamy's 1991 report from Vukovar. "It was like a scene from an apocalyptic mediaeval painting: aboard the trucks was a mess of bloodied, bandaged, wounded humanity, packed four deep, some lying in two inches of icy water that had soaked through the canvas."[17] *Plus ca change*. The difference of the century *passé*, though, was that so effective were MacGahan's reports that they actually helped to bring into being the autonomous state of Bulgaria two years later. It would be gratifying for any modern writer or photographer to emulate his achievement but, as I have said, the effectiveness and immediacy of modern visual communication has effectively innured the armchair consumer of news to such awfulness. Even before the advent of modern communications, Martha Gellhorn was worried about the efficacy of her Second World War reports. "For all the good our articles did, they might have been written in invisible ink, printed on leaves, and loosed to the wind."[18]

What you can have, of course, is a contributory effect on the general passage of events. Photographer Hassan Amini put the point particularly movingly, for those of us who were there, in St. Vincent's Church in Caythorpe, Lincolnshire, at the funeral of his colleague Paul Jenks, "Today Croatia has its independence thanks to the governments and the people who saw Paul's photographs and those of other photographers." That was not to overstate the influence an accomplished photographer can have. Cecil Beaton's 1940 front cover for *Life* - of an injured three year-old girl - is widely credited with having influenced US opinion on joining the war.

And you find yourself drawn back to it all. "I'm gradually getting away from the idea of war but it's still calling me," Don McCullin admitted after his 'retirement.' "After all, if you've been a serious drinker, you still get those terrible thirsty days . . . "[19]. There is that desire to experience the extremes, to live on the brink, to see it simply because it is there and because it is happening. To be a witness. To know yourself better. Like John Le Carré's Honourable Schoolboy. "Sometimes . . . you go in order to remind yourself that survival is a fluke. . . In order to know himself: the Hemingway game. In order to raise his threshold of fear. Because in battle, as in love, desire escalates. When you have been machine-gunned, single rounds seem trivial. When you've been shelled to pieces, the machine gunning's child's play . . ."[20] Of course, no man, physical combatant or journalist or photographer, believes that he will be the next casualty. Death or injury is something that happens to the other chap. In the firing line we all believe we are immortal.

But, additionally, there is the awe-ful realisation that you can actually enjoy, physically and mentally, the heat of battle, the taste of fear and the actuality of survival. And, as a writer, you realise that the extremes of emotion, to which you are so brutally and suddenly exposed, release the ability to string together the words in a way you hitherto hardly dreamt possible. Herbert Matthews identified this process of cause and effect. "If you have not seen a battle, your education has been somewhat neglected - for, after all, war has been one of the primary functions of mankind, and unless you see men fight you miss something fundamental."[21] This is a variation on the more recent observation of Askold Krushelnycky, writing specifically of the appeal of the Croatian conflict to journalists, adventurers and others. "War is a perverse activity, so it is little surprise that it attracts plenty of bizarre characters - some who want to join in, others merely voyeurs. Perhaps everyone who reports on war is in part sating their own dark curiosities. I know I will return soon."[22]

This goes some way to identifying a more suspect motivation which is dangerous and, even, borders on the immoral: a sort of *schadenfreude* which can all too easily become the motivating force. Its most extreme manifestation was probably in some of the mercenaries to be seen on the battlefields of Croatia. Some were clearly there simply for the high which came from inflicting death and damage from a position of wholly imaginary moral high ground. But there is just as much danger in this for the observer as the participant. A war is essentially the ambulance chaser's ultimate dream. The visions of misery and suffering can also provide a convenient reference point for putting aside one's own damaged emotions. Once you're damaged yourself you can take on board a lot of other people's.

There again, it may all be somewhat less cerebral. It was Samuel Johnson who, more than two centuries ago, identified that most enduring of delusions: "Every man thinks meanly of himself for not having been a soldier." Some war correspondents have discovered their own method of dealing with that problem. As Nora Ephron put it in *New York* magazine, "Unlike fighting in the war itself, unlike big-game hunting, working as a war correspondent is almost the only classic male endeavour left that provides physical danger and personal risk without public disapproval and the awful truth is that for correspondents, war is not hell. It is fun."

2. ON THE SUNNY SIDE OF THE ALPS

It all began in Slovenia. June 26 1991 and it was Independence Day. Smallest - and most prosperous - of the seven republics making up the Yugoslav federation, two million Slovenes had voted to go it alone in their tiny state. Bordered to north, east and west by Austria, Hungary and Italy, the Slovenes saw - and continue to see themselves - clearly as mainstream Europeans "on the sunny side of the Alps", as the tourist brochures like to put it. The mouse that roared, was how the more cynical of the Western press were to put it. But, nevertheless, theirs was to be the story of the mouse that roared - and got away with it.

Slovenes had never really regarded themselves as properly belonging to the Yugoslav federation, a hasty creation of the Treaty of Versailles after the First World War. They had always taken a pride in their own language, a distinct cultural identity, the political and social consensus and the homogeneity which characterised their little republic. On December 23 1990 the referendum on independence for Slovenia had produced a vote in excess of 90% in favour. Probably the most efficient and prosperous of the republics making up the crumbling federation, Slovenia, with less than 9% of the population, was producing more than 30% of the hard currency exports. Located at the crossroads of Europe, the Slovenes had lost any ability to identify with an ailing, divided and bankrupt federation hastily cobbled together after the First World War.

The origins and development of that ill-starred federation explain something of what was about to happen in the Balkans. Complex, internecine and atavistic, most observers from any distance find it virtually impossible to unravel the background to the present conflict. A simplified, if not simplistic, outline might run something like this. The 1918 creation of the Kingdom of Croats, Slovenes and Serbs brought together a group of peoples in the Balkans in a way that was

46

geographically and administratively convenient for its progenitors at the Treaty of Versailles. The First War itself had had its origins in Sarajevo, capital of Bosnia Herzegovina with the assassination of the Austrian Archduke Ferdinand by a member of the Young Bosnia movement. In 1878 Austria had occupied Bosnia, and then annexed it in 1908, thus extending its control southwards through Croatia and Slovenia. The Ottomans had taken Bosnia and Herzegovina as long ago as the second half of the 15th century but, over the centuries, competing spheres of influence had continually altered the balances of power and possession in the Balkans with Greece, Turkey, Austria Hungary and Bulgaria all participating in bloody interventionism. The assassination not only brought about the end of the Austro Hungarian empire which had dominated the northern part of the Balkan region for so long, but, in early course, plunged the whole of Europe into war. A long term solution to the fractious Balkan problem was not so much sought by the Versailles peacemakers as the imposition of a bulwark against a German Magyar power bloc: a physical obstacle to influence in the Balkans and the prevention of any future alliance which could have stetched from Baltic to Adriatic. The Versailles answer to this problem was the effective creation of a Greater Serbia to be called Yugoslavia. But this convenient agglomeration of Serbs, Croats, Slovenes, Macedonians and Montenegrins was an explosive ethnic and religious mix destined to last only for some seventy years.

The creaky start was ominous enough. Catholic Croat and orthodox Serb had long deeply distrusted each other. The Croats boycotted the passage of the 1921 constitution. During the 1920s and '30s the Serbs imposed their own version of the Serbo-Croat language, including the use of Cyrillic script used in Serbia. The Croats had always used the Latin version. Parliamentary rule was abolished in Belgrade in 1929 and Yugoslavia came under the direct rule of the Serbian King Alexander. In 1934 he was assasinated by extreme right wing Croats - *ustase* - in the south of France. The Second World War brought about a German occupation of Yugoslavia with the exception of Croatia and parts of Bosnia. An independent Croatian state was allowed by Hitler under the leadership of

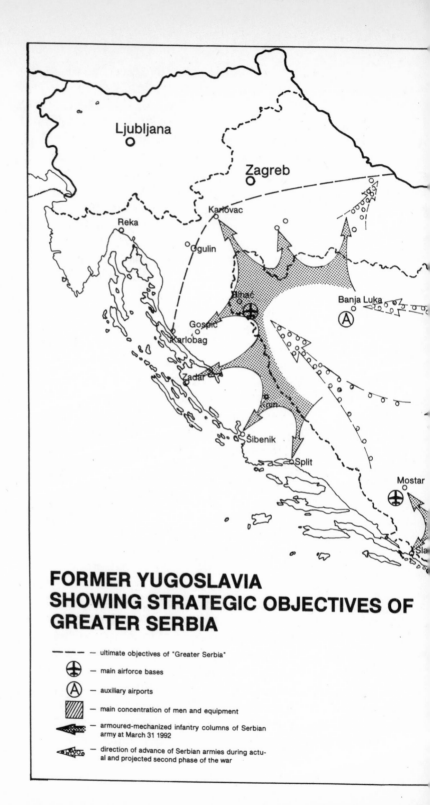

FORMER YUGOSLAVIA SHOWING STRATEGIC OBJECTIVES OF GREATER SERBIA

Ljubljana

Zagreb

Karlovac

Reka

Ogulin

Bihać

Banja Luka

Gospić

Karlobag

Zadar

Knin

Šibenik

Split

Mostar

– – – — ultimate objectives of "Greater Serbia"

— main airforce bases

— auxiliary airports

— main concentration of men and equipment

— armoured-mechanized infantry columns of Serbian army at March 31 1992

— direction of advance of Serbian armies during actual and projected second phase of the war

48

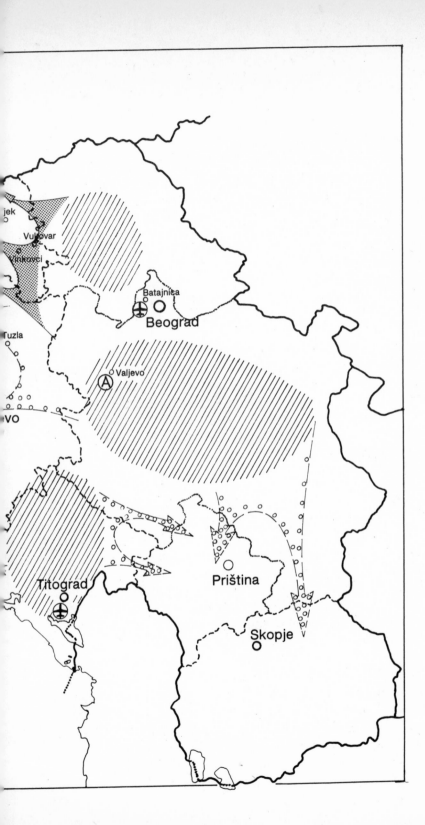

jek

Vukovar

Vinkovci

Tuzla

VO

Batajnica

Beograd

Valjevo

Ⓐ

Titograd

Priština

Skopje

Ante Pavelic and his *ustase* supporters. Unspecified large numbers of Serbs were massacred in the years that followed.

The end of the war brought the only period of peace that Yugoslavia was to know under the iron rule of partisan hero Marshall Josip Tito, himself Croatian by birth. This peace and apparent unity was, in reality, held together by the firm and uncompromising grip of a militarised police state in which any opposition to the Tito regime was ruthlessly suppressed. Tito himself realised that this was the only way to keep the warring factions apart: the personality cult he skilfully developed throughout the state was not to be superceded by any sort of narrow, nationalist ambition. In 1980 Tito died - without an effective heir and leaving behind the impractical system of a rotating presidency.

Throughout the '80s cracks in the framework manifested themselves. There were riots in the Albanian populated province of Kosovo (1981) and the Serbian political and military leadership took an increasingly violent line against the majority Muslim Albanian population over the course of the next decade. Muslim leaders were arrested in Bosnia (1983) - including the man who to become its first President in 1992, Alija Izetbegovic. In the ethnically Hungarian province of Vojvodina, local leaders were replaced by hardline Serbs. The status of the Macedonian language was rejected by Belgrade who declared it to be simply a dialect of Serbian. And the Slovenes became increasingly restless at these extreme displays of Serbian nationalism. In 1989, the Slovene assembly amended the constitution to allow for independence. The genuine wish at that time was for independence within a confederation but Slovenia was not able over the ensuing two years to reach any sort of accord with Belgrade. Total independence became the only option and on June 25 this was declared by both Slovenia and Croatia.

My idea had been to attend the independence celebrations on the evening of June 26. But from lunchtime the Adria Airways flight kept getting put back and put back at Heathrow. There was no indication of trouble that afternoon but, in the early evening, Marilyn, the Adria representative at Heathrow, whispered in my ear. "Keep it to yourself but the military have siezed Ljubljana airport. There are tanks on the runway."

By midnight, most of the passengers for the flight had drifted away. A group of elderly Saga holidaymakers had been persuaded to leave for home, complete with zimmers and sticks. War zones really wouldn't have been suitable for them. Businessmen who had missed their appointments had abandoned their trips. By the time the flight was eventually called at 1 a.m. there was myself, a colleague, half a dozen returning Slovenes and the chief reporter and a photographer from the *Daily Mail*. Our destination was now Zagreb, capital of neighbouring Croatia, also one day into independence: in normal times just a couple of hours drive from Ljubljana.

Arrival at 4 a.m. local time seemed more like arriving back in Britain on the red eye from New York than completing a short European flight. An hour up the road by coach and dawn was breaking. We came to a halt. The line of traffic stretched far ahead up the road. I decided to take a look. I walked for twenty minutes or so past hundreds of stationary vehicles and found a checkpoint at a junction.

There was a handful of armed soldiers and policemen. The thing I noticed first were the fresh new blue, white and red badges on their sleeves and forage caps: three stars and the three Alpine peaks of Triglav - Slovenia's highest mountain - had replaced the single red star of Yugoslavia. Neither English nor German was understood so Eurolengo was brought into use: the odd word of Slovenian punctuated by a mixture of words from various European languages tried in rotation. It's a bit long winded as a method of communication but it generally works out. Anyway, I might as well not have bothered. They didn't know why they had stopped the traffic - just acting on orders - and then, as if on a whim, they decided to restart everything.

But 20km. or so up the road things came to a lasting halt. A massive roadblock made up of heavy lorries had been laid across the highway near Trebnje. Not just one or two lorries but dozens and dozens laid end to end and side by side.

51

Surprisingly well armed troops in brand new camouflage uniforms turned all the traffic back. Returning whence we came, it soon became clear that roadblocks were going up all along the road and not only could we not proceed but we could not go back either. What we did not know then was that in the early hours of that morning tens of thousands of young men - volunteer members of the as yet untried Slovene Defence Force - were being mobilised and were making their way to predetermined strategic locations. Some were setting up roadblocks and checkpoints like the ones we were now encountering, others were simply melting away into the woods and the mountains.

Courtesy of a passing train stopping at a country station we ultimately arrived in Ljubljana at 8 a.m. I had made, I suppose, more than 50 visits to Ljubljana but the atmosphere that morning was like nothing I had experienced before: a mixture of anxiety and purposefulness. The physical evidence of this was taking root all around. Throughout the outskirts of the city roadblocks were being thrown up. Lorries, buses, loads of sand and gravel, gas canisters and bulldozers were being used to seal off streets, motorway exits and important buildings. One word on everyone's lips was to become familiar over the next few days: *blockaade*. Switching on the nine o'clock news, the reason for this was apparent. Film taken earlier that morning showed tanks leaving barracks in Ljubljana and nearby Vrhnika, crushing private cars and smashing through local, hastily improvised barricades.

Thursday was a day of phoney war. The Federal army moved on the airports and border crossing points with tanks and helicopter assault troops. The citizens of Slovenia prepared for battle. Civilians manned the barricades and roadblocks. Motorways were closed and entry and exit ramps blocked. Police set up checkpoints on the smaller roads. The Slovene Defence Force mobilised, donned its brand new Singapore made camouflage uniforms and melted away into the woods and mountains ready to take on the enemy with the Swiss style defence tactics which were to prove so successful.

52

Within the city itself there was a curious calm that day. A small military training aircraft flew repeatedly over the streets dropping leaflets by the thousand. Hastily photocopied and curiously naive, they assured us that resistance was useless and that surrender was the only course.

Sitting at a pavement cafe in Ljubljana just after seven in the evening a military helicopter flew overhead. A few minutes later there was an explosion like a clap of thunder. After hovering near to the parliament building, it had been downed by the Defence Force - complete with its cargo of bread.

The calm of Thursday was followed by Bloody Friday. News was coming in of the attacks on the border posts on the Hungarian and Austrian borders. Our plane was due to take off from Brnik Airport at 10.30. There was clearly no chance. But we decided to try and get to the airport anyway. As we approached the airport at 10.15 two ageing Galeb jets swooped down from the sky, in one single low level run, and unleashed rockets and machine cannon.

I walked up the wooded road to the airport past abandoned road blocks together with a photographer from *Agence France Presse*. All was strangely quiet in the aftermath of the attack. Although we were unaware at the time, on one side of us in the forest were the Slovene Defence Forces and, on the other, hidden in the trees, were the Federal tanks. The airport appeared to be totally deserted apart from its fire brigade which dousing a line of cars destroyed in the car park. Police and military jeeps lay abandoned exactly where they had been at the time of the attack: doors wide open and keys still in the ignition.

We wandered around at will. The Airbus A-230 we were to fly home on was still in its hangar, drilled down the length of the roof with a neat line of holes. Climbing inside, you could see the sky through the neat holes in the superstructure and the gaping holes in the roof of the hangar. The oxygen masks dangled uselessly down. Two Dash 7s were damaged; firemen were extinguishing a fire which had caught on the wings of one standing on the tarmac. Torn and twisted metal and broken glass were everywhere underfoot.

Over at the airport hospital, the medical superintendent held up a 23 mm. machine cannon shellcasing. "Take a look at the first bullet fired in the Third World War!" he joked sardonically.

As we left the airport it was starting to fill up with the world's press. A paramilitary style safari jeep roared up at speed. Painted in army colours and with wire grilles over the windows, we nervously wondered on whose side were the occupants. At closer quarters, amidst a screaming of tyres, the Vienna registration allayed our initial fears.

"Hey man, where's all the action?" enquired the driver. I directed him to the Adria hangar.

"Wanna lift?" We didn't but before I could answer a Czech TV crew passed at speed. "They're coming back! They're coming back!" they shouted. We made for the woods and the Austrians carried on.

We took cover in the woods amidst a crackle of small arms fire. Nearby there were some burned out buses, still smoking. We reckoned they had been fired on by tanks. Later there was an explosion in the direction of the runway. We didn't investigate. We didn't even look. For Nick Vogel and Norbert Werner - the Austrian journalists - their reporting days were over, courtesy of a ground to ground missile fired by a tank from out of the woods. The single missile totally destroyed their jeep immolating them instantly. It wasn't safe enough to recover the bodies for two days.

Meantime, Federal Mig jets were attacking the roadblock at Medvedjek down on the highway to Zagreb; border traffic at Sentilj up on the Hungarian border was also under attack; and border posts were falling to Federal troops helicoptered in over the barricades. The war for Slovenia was on in earnest.

Ljubljana itself was now the number one destination for the world's press. During the course of that Friday, hundreds of foreign journalists, photographers and broadcasters arrived in the capital. The CNN satellite dish poked its way skywards from a balcony at the Holiday Inn; other broadcasters were setting up edit suites in hotels all over the city. A Sunday newspaper asked me to take my exclusive pictures from the airport to the Reuters bureau which was now based in the Holiday Inn Hotel. There they were processed. I got to jump the lengthening queue for wiring pics by giving them one of my pics of the burning buses near the airport. When I came down to the bar there were my erstwhile travelling companions from the *Daily Mail*. They didn't look too pleased with themselves. They'd been up at Sentilj but had been to early for the action. While they were at Sentilj they missed the Brnik attack. I showed them my pics. They looked even more hacked off. I deemed it wise to make my excuses and leave.

Saturday morning I was physically ill. The churning guts were some sort of delayed reaction I suppose. Steinbeck had the same sort of trouble. "And when you wake up and think back to the things that happened they are already becoming dreamlike. Then it is not unusual that you are frightened and ill." [1] So I was in good company, at least.

I attended a press conference which was addressed by President Milan Kucan, Information Minister Jelko Kacin and Foreign Minister Dimitrij Rupelj. They looked distinctly worried men. That afternoon, I took a look around outside Ljubljana with other journalists. First of all, with some crazy, clueless Hungarians, then with a taciturn Greek radio reporter (maybe he just couldn't speak much English, on second thoughts) and, in the early evening, with some Danish pressmen. My hotel- the Slon - and the Holiday Inn were both packed full of press, radio and TV men. I reckoned there must be at least 500 in the city by now with more arriving by the hour. By early evening, though, the police and military were closing off the centre of the city making any sort of movement virtually impossible. The locals were all off the streets and it was vital to wear your press card prominently even to walk a hundred metres down the pavement. Activity outside the parliament building - special forces men with light armoured vehicles and armed plain clothes men - suggested that a secret session had been convened.

That night was tense and restless with sleep punctuated by light machine gun fire. A policeman died in the street outside our hotel. Fears of a fifth column swept the city. Breakfast on Sunday was interrupted by the wail of air raid sirens at nine o'clock precisely, the expiry time of the Federal ultimatum to the leaders of Slovenia. A bit too neat on the old timing I thought. Although I recalled reading that the Russians attacked Finland at nine o'clock one December morning in 1939. Martha Gellhorn observed at the time, "War started at nine o'clock promptly." [2] I hoped that the Yugoslav Federal forces weren't using the same manual.

Everyone went down to the shelters. Except the British, of course. We stood defiantly in the middle of the deserted streets staring boldly into the sky as a few TV crews and photographers warily patrolled the streets. The all clear was sounded at 10.20 and those who had elected for the shelters emerged blinking into the daylight.

The streets of the city were still eerily quiet. Virtually everybody except journalists seems to be at home, waiting, hoping. Bars, restaurants and shops are all closed. There are just a few curious kids on the streets. In the deserted centre of Ljubljana, I see a boy scaling the statue of the national hero, poet and lawyer France Preseren. Young Mateuz Korosec thrusts the new Slovenian tricolour flag into Preseren's bronzed hand, turns and raises his clenched fist in victory salute.

The effect of the morning's air raid alarm on the civilian population was not apparent until, that afternoon, I visited Slovenian friends in their home. For the older members of the family, simply hearing the air raid warnings that morning had constituted a traumatic event in itself. For them the ominous wailing brought back the forgotten memories of another war and were to bring the painful return of nightmares and sleepless nights. They were also upset by the CNN coverage of the war. On the one o'clock news the local anchorman in town to cover the war of the week, had described President Milan Kucan as "a Balkan operator". This tactless observation does not go down well locally.

56

The afternoon press conference has been moved to a larger theatre due to pressure of numbers - and the new one, significantly, is deep underground. The plainclothes bodyguards for the President and for Defence Minister Janez Jansa - he is now dressed in military uniform - have been replaced by heavily armed special forces officers with M6 carbines and snub-nosed machine guns. I shudder to think at the sort of damage they would wreak in the confined space underground.

The leaders of Slovenia all look grey and fatigued that Sunday at the televised press conference. President Milan Kucan has the air of the elder statesman: dapper, firm and decisive. Foreign Minister Dimitrij Rupelj comes over very much as the urbane, shrewd and calculating member of the team. Information Minister Jelko Kacin, youthful and quick witted, chairs the press conferences. He is always in command despite the pressures and only twice that I noted lost his *sang froid*: once with the man from *The Guardian*, who accuses the leadership of dreaming up Sunday's threatened air raid for propaganda reasons, and another time with the correspondent from the radical Slovenian magazine *Mladina*, who wants to know where the money has come from to defend the new republic.

The member of the team who seems the odd man out is Defence Minister Janez Jansa. He seems strangely shy, hesitant and reserved. I later learn that this is not a true impression of the man who was, in effect, an important catalyst in the drive to independence. In 1988, he had been involved in the publication in *Mladina* of secret Federal army plans to take over Slovenia in the event of implementation of moves to independence. He was arrested, tried and imprisoned by a military court - becoming something of a martyr in the process. During the trial a burgeoning human rights movement took to the streets in protest against the Federal authorities. In the martyr came the natural choice for a Defence Minister.

The effort and planning which had gone into the defence of the newly independent republic was necessarily unknown at that time. It was only later in the year - in October - when I talked with Jansa that this became clear to me. The attack on Slovenia

- so sudden, dramatic and unexpected to a world which had expected the Croatian tinderbox to erupt first - had been anticipated by the Slovene leadership since perusal of intelligence reports on May 15. Consequently, for some six weeks before independence a specially appointed commission had prepared for the conflict.

On Monday I do start to wonder. "What am I doing here?" Yet I sense that my Slovenian friends seem to appreciate my inexplicably reassuring foreign presence in their tiny isolated country. Only half of me wanted to leave.

Militarily, things seemed to be improving. We drove for an hour or so down to the village of Crni Vrh where the military had abandoned an ammunition dump. Although they had blown it up, causing enormous damage to roofs and windows throughout the village, everybody seemed vastly encouraged by the army pull out. Incredibly, by early evening, virtually every roof was repaired and every window replaced by the locals and an army of volunteers. The local Defence Corps had captured the fleeing Federal soldiers. But they were most proud of another captive: a dog escaping with the soldiers. A real Federal dog as a prisoner. Much hilarity all round.

Early on Tuesday morning the situation seemed to be approaching a stalemate, and I knew that if I allowed the day to take over and saw my friends again, I would hang on in Ljubljana indefinitely, so I took a taxi to the crowded station feeling confused and emotional about leaving. All the trains out were full. I attached myself to a sealed carriage full of schoolchildren leaving for Zagreb airport, three hours or so away by train. Aged from 12 to 15 they were en route to summer school in Brighton and Hastings. They were excited and happy to leave - except the defiant older boys. They simply wanted to stay - and to fight if required.

Around 1030, as we approached the Croatian border, there were ominous puffs of smoke in the trees a mile or more from the train. I dismissed all sorts of dramatic possibilities from my mind. In the event, a tank offensive on Slovenia was just starting.

At Zagreb airport at midday we were less than two hours from boarding the 'plane. Then a commotion. And then an announcement. "The Federal Army has taken over the airport. It is now closing." Some people started to cry. The lady in charge of the schoolchildren was shepherding them onto a bus. An English voice I recognised from Ljubljana was phoning a story: "Federal army Russian-built T74 tanks are moving on the airport ... Antonov 24 twin turbo prop military transport 'planes are landing ..." John works for *Soldier of Fortune Magazine*.

John and I team up. I persuade him to temporarily relinquish his monopoly on the telephone booth and phone the news editor of a British tabloid. The airport is being evacuated around me and I have one eye on the access road expecting to see tanks emerging at any moment. Getting a line is bad enough. Hanging on for somebody to answer the news desk phone is worse. Then there follows one of those irritating conversations.

"Yes, the military have closed Zagreb airport and tanks are reported to be moving in. Just over an hour ago tank columns attacked Slovenia. What do you mean you can't commission a piece?" Yugoslavia has moved off the front page.

Buses have thoughtfully been provided to get everyone back into Zagreb. But the rout is orderly enough for everyone to be charged for their involuntary evacuation.

Zagreb turns out to be a temporary haven. On the TV we can see tanks are breaking out from the barracks in the city, through crowds of angry locals, and they are rumoured to be surrounding the city.

We see Croatian militia occupying the bridges carrying rail and road traffic into the city. A column of military ambulances is stopped on a bridge at Most Mladosti. The Federal army driver in the escort vehicle has been shot dead by a Croatian with a hunting rifle. There is a neat round hole in his forehead. A stand-off situation between the local militia and the Federals exists.

The Croatian National Guard let us onto the bridge to observe the situation but tell us not to move. They disappear. And we move up to the column. I ask a soldier with his back to us if we can take photographs but when he turns around am considerably disconcerted to see the red star of the Federal forces on his helmet. The Croatians are now levelling their automatic weapons from behind a sandbagged barricade at the side of the bridge. We make our excuses and gingerly leave.

We resolve to get out the next day and stay overnight in The Esplanade, a hotel of 19th century opulence ($186 a night) because it has the best shelter in the city. There are just eight people staying in the enormous hotel.

The next day the news is all of tank columns coming from Belgrade. Zagreb braces itself for attack. We gather other Brits around us: a party of three publishers I know from London and Cherry, a Zagreb born Canadian citizen. We all decide to leave for Belgrade by train. It means going further into Croatia and then crossing into Serbia but we reckon it is safer. The British consul in Zagreb advises us to flee to Hungary.

From the train, columns of tanks can be seen heading north to Slovenia and Croatia. The comforting thing is, according to John, that large numbers of them are either broken down or out of fuel. The train passes through the Slavonia region of Croatia. All is quiet in the pretty towns and villages. We stop for a while at the attractive city of Osijek with its stuccoed Baroque architecture. You would never have guessed at what was but weeks away.

In Belgrade life seems remarkably normal apart from the queues at the filling stations. The National Hotel near the airport is something of a culture shock after the Esplanade. For a start, the room is $156 dollars a night cheaper. But I'm also sharing it with the local wild life. The mosquitoes aren't friendly. In the smoky bar downstairs hookers in leather miniskirts with thighs like tree trunks display their wares to a crowd of appreciative lorry drivers. Cherry tells me the next morning that her friends in Belgrade are shocked to hear where we are staying. It seems

60

to be well known as a sex and drug dealers' hangout. I missed out on the action.

The 7 a.m. TV news on Thursday has a very short political piece relating to the war and, bafflingly, a four minute news special on the pigeon problem in Belgrade. At the airport my APEX ticket for the flight on the previous Friday's shot-up Adria plane is disdainfully refused by JAT, the Yugoslavian 'national' carrier and I am obliged to stump up $420 for a *return* ticket to Belgrade. The only other option was a single at $650.

When I turned up to use the return portion of the JAT ticket from Heathrow to Belgrade at the end of July there was no record of my booking. The flight was overbooked and I was bumped off it. So I bought another return from yet another airline . . .

THE WAR IN SLOVENIA

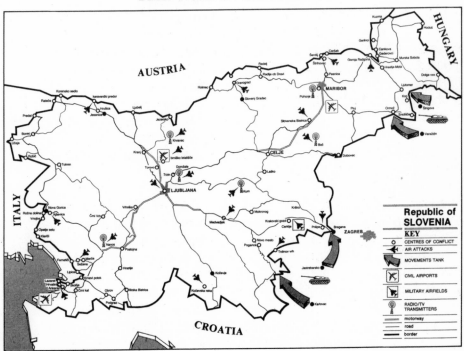

3. THE HIGHWAY TO HELL

I used to congratulate myself that I was not naive enough to expect war to be like a John Wayne movie. In reality, I discovered it was. And for a brief few days in September I found myself in a supporting role, if not a star actor, in a bizarre black farce enacted in devastated eastern Croatia. That same sort of mixture of tragedy and humour must have been in mind for Mark Twain when he observed, "The secret source of humour itself is not joy but sorrow."

The Press Centre for the war is in the plush and incongruous surroundings of Zagreb's Intercontinental Hotel. Of a morning, journalists mill about questioning the bright and earnest young men and women - most are Croatians who have come back from places like Australia and America. The pressmen plan their days at the front or, possibly for those with more sense, at the two press conferences and in the bar. There is a bizarre holiday atmosphere as guides and interpreters are arranged.

"Hey, Miroslav, it's your lucky day - you've drawn CNN today!" Miroslav doesn't look over the moon about his assignment. Possibly because the CNN crews are known as the highest risk-takers in a war which, just in the first three months, had claimed the lives of twelve journalists, with two more missing without trace.

There's no interpreter for me today. This is bad news. Although I'm prepared to take the odd risk or two, one personal rule I have is not to travel without a native speaking Croatian. So it looked like a day with the press pack at the conferences and watering holes. But, lo, Sherry sweeps in.

Now American lady journalists do tend to look like movie stars and Sherry - from Iowa - is no exception. Manicured, designer dressed, dripping with jewels, made up (warpainted?) and bubblingly effervescent she cuts a dazzling swathe through the jean-clad film crew p.a.s. I always talk to Americans. Lacking all that tedious European reserve, the rapport tends to get going quickly and you find things out rapidly (especially from CIA operatives at bars, but that's another story).

And, guess what? Sherry actually speaks Croatian by some fortuitous accident of birth. We two were obviously made for each other and I'm really looking forward to a cosy day out. Then the bad news. She's actually travelling with someone else and I agree to the threesome.

Fortunately, Judy is not the incredible hulk I feared. Rather, a mixture of Marilyn Monroe and Barbie Doll. She's also a complete flake. Which is not what you expect from an actual Professor of Journalism at the University of Texas here to write an intellectual analysis of journalists under fire. As she goes off to spend half an hour in the "bathroom" to engage the mascara I do wonder if she is going to be a bit of a liability, but dismiss the uncharitable thought from my mind.

I knew from Croatian TV there'd been a lot of fighting at the town of Pakrac, normally just a couple of hours drive from Zagreb, and it sounded a reasonable destination. As Rolling Stone writer and foreign correspondent P J O'Rourke put it in his book *Holidays in Hell*, "I just figured what with guns going off and things blowing up, there'd be plenty of deep truths and penetrating insights." [1] So, we're roaring down the completely deserted Zagreb to Belgrade motorway in Mr Hertz's Rentacar when we hit the first major crisis.

"Paul, I need to visit the bathroom!" comes the cry from Judy in the back. Sherry observes, "How does it feel to be out for the day with your two elder sisters?" I desist from comment. I don't have any sisters. And, anyway, I'm older than the girls. But I'm too gallant to brag about my youthful exterior.

A few kilometres down the road in the town of Kutina, where you can already hear the sound of heavy shelling, the bathroom brigade decamp into some stranger's house and I visit the local police headquarters. Now, I'm getting quite good at this.

"Offizeer," you shout. It's very important in war situations to speak to organ grinders and not the monkeys. When he appears you produce every bit of paper you have: passport, press card, driving licence, National Library of Scotland reading room ticket, and so on. He can't read any of this stuff, most likely. There are two words, though, I have found every soldier in the war understands and which invariably wreaths his face with smiles.

"BBC, Lonndonn." I announce. Now, I don't know what the BBC in London might actually think about my taking their name in vain throughout the battle zones of Croatia but, believe you me, it's the best way to actually achieve anything.

The commandant produces his battle map of the area when I ask about the way to Pakrac. Disturbingly large areas are marked 'Chetnik' but he starts to draw a somewhat complicated route. Now I'm the chap who couldn't cope with the complexities of the Italian railroad system last year, never mind wend my way through this lot. However, I have a softly, softly strategy which has always worked for me without fail. Village by village, I work my way to the front line stopping at every bar. That way, you will *always* find out exactly what is going on.

As we leave, Sherry asks some sort of question in Croatian which I don't understand. Just in case she's asking for the local bathroom map, I don't pursue things.

Just down the road we pass - going the other way - the WTN film crew. I wave them down. Somewhat disconcertingly, they simply urge us, "Go back, go back. You can't get to Pakrac ". Now, that sort of defeatist talk is not the way to cover a war. So we press on to the next - shell-shattered - village of Gaj. All the houses are either boarded up or there are gaping holes in walls and roofs. The windows of the local shop are blown out and you can simply walk in where the plate glass once was. The shelves are fully stocked. Enquiries at a small but well patronised bar

14 Going through the lines on the outskirts of Pakrac, September.

15 Devastation, Prekopakrac.

17 VBR 128mm. rocket battery (type M-73), eastern Croatia.

18 The main Zagreb to Belgrade motorway at Novska. In happier times one of Europe's busiest motorways - the main link to Greece, Turkey and beyond. By September, Novska was the end of the line and only stray cattle used the motorway.

16 Defended flatblock, Pakrac.

19 Saturday afternoon in September at the cafe, Jasenovac.

20 War trophy of dubious provenance. A Croatian soldier displays a Serbian Orthodox cross, Bosanski Brod, April.

21 Local people besiege the Federal army barracks at Samobor, September.

22 Resignation. Soldiers and police guard a bridge near Dubica, September.

23 Croatian guardsman, Jasenovac.

4 This M-84 JNA tank was destroyed by 'friendly fire' in the bitterly fought over front line
village of Nustar, just a few kilometres down the road from Vukovar.

25 A T-55 tank joins the battle for the Bosnian town of Modrica, May.

26 T-55 tank, Turanj.

27 Early days of the war. A homemade tank based on a Second War James truck, Dubica.

28 Captured Federal army 128mm. Oganj rocket battery near Pokupsko.

reveal there is one route open to Pakrac and we press on - after finding the obligatory bathroom.

An hour later and we are driving round this forest on roads which would be fine for tractors - even tanks . We are, of course, completely lost. There are a lot of tree trunks laid deliberately across roads and so there's a good bit of reversing and enough thirteen point turns on the narrow tracks to get me through the advanced driving test. I casually ask Sherry about her query to the commandant back in Kutina.

"I just asked him what were our chances of getting through to Pakrac."

"What did he say?"

"Fifty, fifty," she cheerily reported.

Retracing our steps, we come face to face with a convoy of half a dozen cars: spray painted for camouflage and with their windows shot out, weaponry protrudes from every orifice. I recognise a guy from the bar and he makes the sort of offer you can't refuse.

"All around in these woods are Chetniks. If they catch you, kill you and play with the women. You come with us to Pakrac."

And so we commenced a bizarre progress to relieve embattled Pakrac. Our gleaming white VW Golf car in the middle of the convoy - I declined a kind offer on behalf of the Hertz Corporation to spray paint same - we set out on an oddyssey from village to village, collecting men, guns and cars as we went. At every village the form was reassuringly the same: a sort of party by motorcade. A little bit like I imagine a Presidential whistle stop tour. Much backslapping, laughing and joking, uncertain camaraderie and much mutual demonstration of weaponry, apparently dug out from attics and barns. Some of this hardware might have passed as the latest thing in Chicago in the 1930s but it doesn't look to be up to the task in hand. Invariably, there were beers and then a bottle of home made

65

Opposite page:

29 TAM armoured police vehicle in the centre of Ljubljana, June 1991.

slivovich would be handed around from mouth to mouth by way of a fraternal rite. It would have been churlish to refuse.

The girls were obviously making a big hit with the guys and everything was getting rather *macho*. I recall, a trifle disturbingly, the words of the aforementioned Mr O'Rourke, "It will always be more fun to carry a gun around in the hills and sleep with ideology-addled college girls than to spend life behind a water buffalo or rotting in a slum." I am a bit alarmed about Judy's tendency to observe in English how young these guys are and then address them as "Bambino". This they don't seem to appreciate and in view of their assorted weaponry, I find it somewhat tactless. But it's becoming increasingly clear that the girls are my *laisser passer* and I keep my mouth shut.

At one bar, a grinning, moustachioed character asks me to hold out my hand. Thinking it might be another beer, I stretch it out to find a grenade clamped in my palm. I just hold on, grinning furiously, until the beer is finished. Much amusement all round. Meantime, Judy discovers she has run out of film. I tell her, somewhat brusquely, that it's Sunday and the shops are closed. There's the crump of heavy artillery in the background.

By the time we reached a small village - Prekopakrac - on the outskirts of my destination, let's say I was feeling quite brave about things. That was really quite good because it was under constant bombardment. I abandoned the girls when they went to the bathroom and was taken in a fast, bullet-scarred car down into the town. I try not to think too hard about the bullet hole in the windscreen, directly in my line of vision, the shattered glass spreading out in great tentacles over the field of view.

Down in Pakrac there was an awful lot of the grim reality of war around. Nothing had prepared me for the scene of senseless and utter devastation in a town which had then been under attack from the Yugoslav army and Chetnik irregulars for twenty days. Some buildings had totally disappeared into enormous craters caused by heavy artillery; others were pockmarked and holed by machine cannon or rocket attack from the air. All the time there was the sharp 'crack' of sniper attack. Not only was the town surrounded by the Yugoslav federal army who were shelling it, but the Chetnik guerillas were actually inside it; an invisible enemy holed up in flat buildings and literally shooting at anything that moved. More disturbing even was the information gleefully imparted to me by my guide that many of the snipers were Federal Army special forces: crack shots with high power rifles. He handed me a vicious looking bullet of Czech manufacture. Narrow and very pointed, it thickened out disturbingly at the back end - or whatever you call it. This agent of destruction doesn't just enter the body at one point and pass cleanly through on the other side, leaving some sort of neat hole. The hole may be neat enough at the front, but as it spins its way through flesh and bone it tears away a great chunk of the body as it emerges.

There were few defensive positions remaining for the Croat defenders. We went to one modern flatblock on the outskirts of the town. Surrounding blocks were, unpromisingly, shattered by what appeared to be aerial attack. We ran from the car into the block where several flats were still occupied. Not by the normal quota of domestic residents but almost exclusively by what appeared to be a mixture of uniformed soldiers and civilian enthusiasts, all bearing an extraodinary range of weaponry. I was shown the technique of moving about the rooms and stairs: close to walls, at the backs of rooms and at the double past windows and through open areas.

We sat down for the usual beer with pear brandy chaser. A body lay behind the sofa a few yards from where we drank. The talk was all of when the EEC or the UN would come in to relieve the siege. I found it impossible to disillusion these embattled and dedicated men trying desperately to defend their homes. I was embarrassed by their touching faith in the toothless lion of the EEC. Flavia Kingscote clearly felt the same way back in 1941 when she wrote about the German attack on Yugoslavia: "I cannot convey in adequate words the faith, the expectations of those people. I pray they may never be disillusioned and that I may see the day when we justify their confidence in us by actions equally worthy of their trust." [2]

Another hair-raising drive then followed to the centre of military operations at the police station. Whilst I was at the police headquarters a massive barrage started. I had never been under that sort of sustained attack before. It was the coping with the noise which seemed to take over all the senses. Not just the noise of exploding shells all around but, as the Croatians returned fire from the basement with automatic weapons, the deafening confusion of sound was like an anaesthetic which denied all the other senses.

In a lull in the fighting we ran a zigzag course back to the car, punctuated by a mortar which, thankfully, showered us in no more than dust and debris. We left Pakrac at speed. Despite the rain of bullets, mortars and general unpleasantness, incredibly, it seemed to me, we were still alive. All the fire - the snipers excepted - seemed to be totally indisriminate and I mused that most people were killed 'accidentally'. I ruminated on the statistical chances of death in this war. Were you more likely to be killed by accident in this disorganised multi-fronted war than in one of the more regimented variety? The journalistic death toll seemed to suggest so and I closed down this avenue of thought. But, without doubt, I did, that day, take risks that later I would not have taken.

Back in Prekopakrac, the girls had been having a whale of a time. They had been fed, watered and generally entertained royally by the local soldiery. An inquiry from Judy about the nearest shop selling photographic film - I wouldn't have had the nerve - had, incredibly, produced within a matter of minutes a whole box of films salvaged from the ruins of some local emporium. I'm really not too sure about associating with looters. But the death penalty is obviously applied around these parts in a more random fashion. My travelling companions seemed to have taken a shine to the notion of staying overnight. The local head Rambo announced we could stay at his aunt's house. I was not keen. Even less keen when we arrived at a farmhouse in the middle of nowhere with no aunt in evidence. The girls were captivated by the rural solitude. Captivated they certainly would be, I reckoned. After all, a chap fighting in the front line is likely to think it pretty unreasonable of a woman who fails to come across. The girls were appalled at my cynicism about the motives of the 'bambinos'.

The journey back to Zagreb was largely uneventful. Except, ten kilometres up the road, Judy discovered she'd left her mascara in the "bathroom" at Prekopakrac. I declined to go back. Then it did get *really* unpleasant.

Three weeks later I'm doing my couch potato thing back home in safe old Scotland. As I flick idly from channel to channel, I catch the News at Ten and some immortal words to the effect that there followed an exclusive report from the Croatian town of Pakrac. "Besieged for two months, an ITN crew was the first to reach Pakrac as it was relieved by Croatian National Guard." Now, I could have sworn that those were some of the same guys we passed going in the opposite direction. Glad you made it chaps.

4. THE BRIDGE AT POKUPSKO

The column of refugees stretched up the road as far as the eye could see. In their hundreds they came. *Les damnés de la terre.* On the back of tractors, in trailers, in horse-drawn carts and on foot - driving their cattle before them. These were the peasants of central Croatia in full flight, barely 25 km. from the capital of Zagreb, streaming across one of the last escape routes: the bridge at Pokupsko.

Earlier, Federal army tanks had smashed through the Croatian front line at Vidusevac, 15 kilometres further up the road. As the army advanced, followed by the feared Chetnik guerillas, the countryside all around emptied. Croat villagers and peasants salvaged whatever they could of their worldly goods and piled them aboard carts and trailers.

The faces of the children bore expressions of bewilderment and confusion; those of their parents, simple terror. It was desperately clear that for these people their way of life had come to an end. In amongst them were small groups of soldiers in retreat: mud-spattered, exhausted and dejected with a strange hollow look on their faces. Unexpectedly, I saw a face I recognised from a couple of weeks previously - from the detachment which had then just arrived to defend Vidusevac. When I had caught up with the three truckloads of volunteers they were in buoyant mood. Under the command of a young girl called Nena - the first female officer and a veritable veteran in the Croatian National Guard with several months service behind her - the mood was of optimism. Signs for victory; a conviction that retreat was not an option and an eagerness for battle. Now all this young man's optimism and enthusiasm had gone. "I cannot speak about it. It was terrible," was all he could say but his heavy lidded eyes and exhausted features said it all. The boy of twenty or so now looked like a man of forty.

At one end of the surfaced metal bridge a group of Croatian National Guardsmen were laying charges to blow it up while, at the other, Croatian police manned a sandbagged checkpoint collecting aged hunting rifles and battered shotguns from the refugees. Their primitive weaponry was tossed into the backs of trucks and Landrovers for redistribution to newly called-up men in uniform.

It was about 4.30 in the afternoon and the light was starting to go. The stream of refugees still stretched into the distance. I was on one knee in the middle of the bridge juggling with the cameras when the first report was heard. Amidst the urgent shouts from soldiers to take cover, I felt my hair literally parted by heavy artillery shells passing overhead. Then there was the "Crump, crump, crump" of the shells landing in fields around the bridge. One hit a house a couple of hundred yards away. On the bridge itself there was no cover. There seemed to be nothing to do and in any case I was paralysed with fear. But I did have the sense to crouch down lest I was thrown over into the river by the blasts.

The barrage probably lasted for no more than 10 or 15 seconds although it seemed much longer. In its wake came a more immediate danger. A stampede of people, horses, cattle and bulls thundered along the bridge in a confused maelstrom of wailing children, screaming women and urgently shouting menfolk, struggling to control their livestock. We all fled together in a stumbling, jumbled mass of animals and humanity, all driven by the same terror. About a hundred metres away a shell landed on a house and it disappeared in a cloud of smoke and dust. Quite suddenly, I was hauled onto the front of a tractor on which I perched precariously until we reached the village of Pokupsko.

The village itself was crowded with troops and military vehicles who seemed to mill about aimlessly with very little direction. One building sported a flag with a large Red Cross. I thought I would take a look at what appeared to be, to all intents and purposes, the local hospital. This turned out to be naive on my part: either casualties had not yet turned up or the local military command were all sick.

71

On the other side of the village a unit of the Croatian ZNG was hastily setting up a captured lorry-borne Oganj rocket battery. Oganj is Serbo-Croatian for blizzard. Possibly the artillery which had shelled us on the bridge was being targeted. Confusingly - and momentarily alarmingly - they were wearing Yugoslav Federal Army style uniforms but I noted with relief the chequered insignia of Croatia and the initials 'ZNG' plastered on their helmets.

Two refugees who had been on the bridge - an elderly woman dressed in black and her husband in what was clearly his best suit - were making their way disconsolately by, he driving the tractor at a snail's pace while she drove their half dozen cows behind. Their utter desolation was so painfully evident.

"Where are you going?" someone asked.

The woman just shook her head, shrugged her shoulders and replied, *"Ja ne znam"* ("I've no idea").

The lot of a refugee is ever one of the most desperate of straits. But at that moment I wondered about those who were not among the refugees. Those who had either left it too late to flee or had elected to stay. The pattern of human behaviour in villages under threat was invariably the same. The young and the fit, hunting rifle or shotgun in hand, would leave their homes and join the local defence forces. As the battle for the area turned against those volunteers - as it usually did when they were pitted against the heavy armour and artillery of the JNA backed by the Chetniks - they would return home and pile high their carts and trailers. Relatives and children would be loaded aboard and the flight would begin. More often than not, the old and the infirm would stay behind to await an uncertain fate. Either physically unable or simply unwilling to abandon the homes of a lifetime, black shawled women could be seen waiting at the gates and in the gardens of neat homes. Waiting for what they knew not, these belated guardians of a whole way of life which was disappearing, possibly for ever.

Once, in the village of Dubica in central Croatia which was about to be taken by the advancing Chetniks - the Croatian National

72

Guard had already passed in full retreat - the desperate poignancy of the end of a whole way of life for a family was brought home to me. From a neat house at the side of the road a man, maybe in his early '30s, had piled into his small family car his wife, his two young children, suitcases, bedding, dishes, pans - the barest essentials of day to day living at some future destination of which they were unaware. At the gate to their garden the family dog stood a-barking. Now, you certainly couldn't claim to read incredulity on the face of a dog but I could swear I could identify the very moment in time that the faithful family hound realised that it was to be abandoned: that there was simply no room left aboard the small cramped family car. As the laden Yugo drew away from the front gate, and the sound of the Chetnik advance grew ever nearer, man's best friend set off in a desperate pursuit of his owners, pounding along the road with all the power he could summon. But, as the car accelerated away, the dog fell ever farther behind until any hope of keeping up had to be abandoned.

There was a generally unrecognised factor in the the human misery of the refugees of Croatia. In most parts of what was Yugoslavia, building your own home means exactly what the phrase implies. Far removed from the comparatively simple exercise of calling in architect and builder or purchasing a package from a speculative builder, new homes are literally built by their owners, relatives, friends and local labour. The ownership of a home of your own is a dream which, more often than not, is physically laboured for over a period of many years. From the foundations to the roof; the electrics, the plumbing, the joinery; bathrooms, kitchens, bedrooms and living space: all are lovingly and physically created by the future occupants. And all this in so many thousands of instances has either had to be deserted under the duress of war or has simply been blown apart by some random act of shelling or rocketing. Frequently, and understandably, the occupants tend to hang on until the very last moment, unable to take in what is happening to their world, seduced by the apparent security of four walls and a roof. And then, quite suddenly, a mortar or a shell or a rocket will slam into the roof or one of the walls shattering the illusion of safety. Martha Gellhorn observed this thinking in Spain during the Civil War, " . . . you are always safer in your own place, with the things you know. Somehow you do not believe you can get killed when you are sitting in your own parlour, you never think that."[1]

And so people hang on in the apparent security of home. It is then all too easy to leave it too late. Mehmet Husic, a journalist living in the Sarajevo suburb of Dobrinja, telephoned his report to the outside world: "This morning they started to come into Dobrinja. They took some houses, and took the people inside away. I can see their tanks on the street outside. The Serbs are destroying the area and killing people. From my window I can see the Serbian soldiers going into empty flats. I am very afraid for my wife and daughter. Sooner or later they will find out where we are . . ."[2]

At Brest, a few kilometres from Pokupsko, a family had hung on until armageddon had finally made its appearance in this sudden and apocalyptic manner. On the first floor balcony of a house with its roof stripped bare of tiles and its interior destroyed, the washing was still hung out to dry: a red tablecloth, a pair of blue jeans, some white sheets, all flapping idly in a light breeze on a warm October day. Further down the road was a line of once neat, modern houses. Every one was damaged in some way. Shells or mortars had destroyed roofs and walls. The occupants were all gone and their place was now taken by men in rough and ready uniforms. These men were from Petrinja, across the river, now taken by the Chetniks. Soldiers in name only, these men lived in the dank and fetid basements and cellars of the deserted houses in the hope of seeing their own homes once again. But they were now effectively front line troops - in indefensible positions - in somebody else's home. The chickens, the pigs and much of the other livestock had been abandoned by the occupants of Brest in their haste to flee. At least this gave those new dispossessed occupants a source of food; there was also plenty of home made wine and brandy to drink and wood for a fire. "But they might have left us some of their women," one wryly observed. And all they could see as they sheltered there was the black smoke day after day as the Chetniks burned Petrinja.

74

Meantime, in a field at the edge of Pokupsko an elderly couple were frantically gathering in the last of the harvest and loading it onto a trailer. Behind us there was the "Whoosh, whoosh, whoosh" of rockets from a lorry-borne launcher searing their way into the darkening sky. The peasants in the fields did not even look up from their work. The prosecution of a war they did not understand was of considerably less importance than the gathering in of the final harvest. But, I could not help reflecting, in the killing fields of Croatia, where fleeing civilians were fair game for the military men, there was a grim reaper of quite another kind abroad.

When the photographs were processed some of the images of the fleeing refugees were quite striking. Of all the drama and panic on the bridge itself there was little except a confused mass of bodies and a lot of images of legs moving at the double. Many of the pictures, especially those shot in black and white, could have been taken fifty years previously as Belgian and French peasants fled the Nazi onslaught and I dimly recalled the recollections of a newsreel cameraman back in 1940. At home I found the book.

"They were old and young, fit and sick, yet one thing was common to them all. The frightened stare in their eyes. . . What can one do to stop this sort of thing? I kept asking myself, as yet more refugees straggled past. There was only one answer - film as many of these atrocities as possible." [3]

Plus ca change. When war comes, when politicians and generals seek to change borders, shift frontiers and move their pieces like on some deadly games board, it is those ordinary people whose lives are irrevocably changed. After the Second World War Martha Gellhorn wrote, "When you shift a frontier it means that a man with two cows and two children and a wife and a little plot of land, and another man who owns a small shop where he sells wine or shoes or pills or writing paper, will feel the change."[4] Populations do not suddenly demand war en masse. They respond to the persuasion of politicians; the demands of the Big Lie. In Slovenia, young Federal troops had been denied access to newspapers, radio or television and,

despatched to sieze the border posts, had been told that
Yugoslavia was under attack from the Austrians. In Croatia, the
Serbian leadership claimed attempts to create a Fourth Reich
from Baltic to Adriatic. And the Croatian leaders arguably
plunged into war having failed to put into place adequate
protection for the Serbian minority.

It is, then, for ordinary people to reap the whirlwind of war.
There are incalculable costs in war which only the direct victims
experience. How do you assess damage - personal, emotional
and privately economic - which can never fit into a neat column
of figures? This was the sort of damage which was so visible
that day. Those particular refugees of war are themselves now
an unidentifiable and vanished part of a vast Croatian diaspora
of more than one and a half million. Their fates are now as
unclear as their misery was apparent on the bridge at Pokupsko.

AREAS OF THE REPUBLIC OF CROATIA
UNDER PROTECTION OF UNPROFOR

The total area of eastern and western Slavonia, together with Krajina, is approximately 12.000 km² and com-
prises 21,4% of the Republic of Croatia's territory.

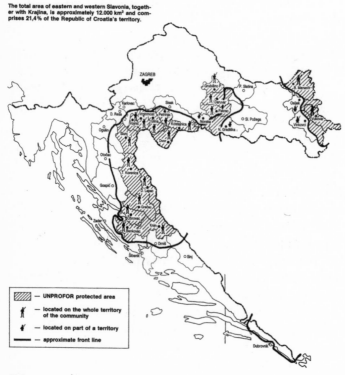

76

5. NOT SO QUIET ON THE EASTERN FRONT

It was in the warm autumn of the war that I discovered the road - indeed the only road - to the hotly disputed eastern frontline. Whilst the attention of the world was transfixed in that last week of October by the threat to the ancient city of Dubrovnik and its historic buildings, a massive attack was being stepped up on Croatia's strategically more important eastern front in Slavonia.

In strategic terms, Dubrovnik, on the Adriatic coast at the very southern tip of Croatia, was of negligible importance. There was no concentration of troops or armaments in the city and the only soldiers there were lightly armed irregulars defending their own 'patch'. A well meaning shipborne influx of Croatian artists and intellectuals, who dubbed themselves "Citizens of Dubrovnik", and who were led by Federal president Stipe Mesic, helped to ensure that worldwide media attention was focused on Dubrovnik. This must, in the short term at least, have been a situation which brought much comfort to those Serbian generals and political leaders prosecuting the war from Belgrade. In the long term, however, the television images of modern shells bouncing off the walls of the ancient Adriatic city were themselves to rebound on the aggressors.

The new eastern offensive was launched by the Federal Army (JNA) using a devastating combination of heavy artillery and multiple rocket launchers. Mig jets joined the fray the following day. The immediate objectives were to further pound the beleagured cities of Osijek and Vukovar and, at the same time, these tactics were intensified against Vinkovci, 15 kilometres to the south of Vukovar. Vinkovci had been shelled several times a day for many weeks but, that weekend, a sustained attack was launched with the objective of dislodging the Croatian National Guardsmen who remained to defend the town.

When I arrived on the Saturday morning, most of the civilian inhabitants had left and the streets were eerily deserted. The only place of semi-normal activity left in the town was the bar of the Hotel Slavonija, a modern, recently built establishment. A few windows were broken, otherwise things looked pretty normal. Inside, it was going like a fair. The Kalashnikovs were stacked in the foyer like umbrellas on a rainy day. The bar itself was full of smoke, noise and bravado. A television blasted out the war reports to an accompaniment of cheers or jeers, depending on the news. Lord Carrington was wittering on about coming back to Yugoslavia "to knock people's heads together", as if they were rather unpleasant cads on the playing fields of Eton. A striking black haired girl in camouflage uniform served the drinks from behind the bar: the glasses were emptied as fast as they hit the counter. I asked a chap who looked as though he might be an officer if he wasn't concerned that most of his men appeared to be quite hopelessly drunk. "Not at all," he averred in a relaxed manner. "Other side all drunk as well."

The owner of the hotel was still displaying the American Express sign. And the room rate was pretty good at around £6.00 a night. Hardly the Ritz, but I booked myself and my driver into the establishment.

We asked a couple of locals in the street outside if "it was quiet around here". They looked quite baffled. Maybe they don't understand us, I thought. Later that day I understood why they had looked so uncomprehending.

There were a few battered and bullet-ridden cars speeding soldiers through the empty canyons that had once been busy streets. 'Cars' is probably a misnomer. Mobile colanders would be more accurate. Incredibly, I saw two soldiers on motorbikes wearing British army uniforms: standard issue but with large Union Jacks sewn onto the upper sleeves.

I was pretty dumbfounded. In the absence of any other more appropriate opening gambit I lamely enquired, "Do you speak English?" Indeed they did - in accents straight out of *Eastenders*

- but they weren't too keen on the exchange of names and addresses routine. Nor photographs. Soldiers of fortune, they maintained they were there for love - not money. Croatia can get you that way. "We've gotta go," they shouted as they roared off. They didn't look to me like the pride of the British army but they were evidently streetwise. They knew something I didn't. A couple of seconds later a shell slammed into the road less than a hundred metres away showering us with lumps of tarmac. All of a sudden I was glad of the protection offered by the Gulf War flak jacket.

Vinkovci must have been a pretty town. It was once home to some 85,000 people. The buildings in the centre were principally 19th century. There was some quite outstanding *art nouveau* architecture, albeit pockmarked by holes and a total absence of windows. The Baroque public buildings in the main square were totally deserted and some were quite shattered. While the world weeps for Dubrovnik, I thought, Vinkovci starts to look like one vast Swiss cheese. It was clear from craters left in the road - some 3-4 feet deep - that the JNA was using heavy artillery, possibly 128 or 155mm. howitzers.

When we arrived, the town was deceptively quiet. Although the streets were empty, the evidence of damage was all around and there was just the heavy crump of distant artillery fire.

It was around 2.30 in the afternoon. We had been told we could probably get to the village of Nustar, a few kilometres up the road to Vukovar. We couldn't find the road to Nustar but an aged peasant on a bicycle obligingly offered to lead us to the road. As we crawled through the deserted streets behind him on the outskirts of the town the bombardment started. Plumes of dark smoke rose from the landscape a kilometre or so ahead. Our guide cycled insouciantly on, quite unperturbed: either so used to the pyrotechnics he was oblivious to them; or simply unimpressed by the long term might of the JNA. My stock Croatian phrase, *"Dali put seguran napred*?" - Is the road ahead safe? - was now clearly as redundant as "My postillion has been struck by lightning.".

We drove out of the town, shells landing in the fields around us. The crackle of light automatic machine guns seemed ominously near. From which side and from where was the sixty-four thousand dollar question. Shells were landing ahead of us and to our rear. This type of attack was demoralising in the extreme: there were the loud bangs of the guns being fired; the waiting for the whistle or the scream of the shell passing overhead; and the paralysing fear that you might not hear the shell passing overhead. You could then be pretty sure it is about to impinge on your world terminally. I recalled war photographer Robert Capa's combat advice, "Stay where you are. If they haven't hit you, they haven't seen you." I wasn't so sure. It seemed to me that we were being bracketed. In the end, we waited for an explosion ahead and then drove through through the stoor of dust and smoke. Great lumps of tarmac littered the road and I was terrified the tyres would puncture. No Kwik Fit around here. In the event, the tarmac was soft from the heat of the explosion and it was, I imagine, like driving through hot toffee.

What we did not know then was that attacks were being launched on the villages of Nustar, to the north, and Murkovci, to the south east, in an attempt to encircle Vinkovci and cut through the Croatian lines, then held right up to the outskirts of Vukovar. These beleagured outposts of the Croatian forces were right up against the republic's eastern border with its Serbian enemy. As the JNA launched its attacks that afternoon, Chetnik guerillas all around were planning to rise up the next day and take large tracts of countryside and attack villages along the road to Zagreb.

Already, that morning, what in happier times was a 200 km. drive taking less than two hours to eastern Slavonia had been a drive of some 400 km., taking more than four hours as we drove around the Chetnik held areas along the single secure main route into the area. Every few kilometres, there were checkpoints where soldiers and police rigorously checked documents. This route was jammed with military vehicles, ambulances, petrol tankers and container trucks hauling all the essentials of war up to the beleagured frontline towns and villages. Later in the week, this route temporarily became

80

impassable. Serbs living around the lifeline rose up and started to mortar the road. The town of Djakovo, 20 km. to the west of the front line, with its vast and beautiful cathedral rising out of the plain, dubbed by one Pope as the most beautiful church between Venice and Constantinople, was mortared and several villages along the lifeline route were attacked with Oganj multiple rocket launchers.

The effect on civilian populations attacked by these weapons is devastating. In just under 60 seconds, 32 128 mm. rockets are launched from a truck mounted battery and slam into their targets, within a concentrated area, without warning in rapid succession. These rocket launching systems can work at a range of up to 28km. The shorter range M-73 rocket launcher, sometimes known as the VBR, is also 128mm. in calibre and can be towed behind most vehicles. It fires a similar number of projectiles but over a shorter effective distance - around 8 km. It was widely used on both sides, especially after the CNG captured large numbers of them from surrendered JNA military barracks.

The top of the range weapon in this particularly fiercesome battery of armament was the Bosnian manufactured Orkan launcher: 262mm. in calibre and delivering 12 rockets in around 30 seconds. It was developed only in the late 1980s by Yugoslavia and possessed many 'refinements' - like delayed explosive potential in missiles fired, posing very real dangers to rescuers, medical teams and others (contrary to the Geneva Convention). Versions of the Orkan, constituent parts of which were clearly manufactured in Yugoslavia, were spotted in 1988 in Iraq, a regime with which Belgrade has had close links. Experimentation with chemical warheads also emerged in the autumn of 1991.

Later the next week, I came upon the evidence of experimentation with chemical weapons. The Orkan rocket launching system had apparently been adapted to deliver chemicals. Evidence reached Zagreb that blister gas experimentation had been carried out near Nova Gradiska and at Visoka Greda, areas with Croatian populations within Serbian held territory. It proved impossible to establish whether or not injury or loss of life had been caused as a result, but radio amateurs were picking up JNA radio transmissions warning Serbian paramilitaries to avoid "contamination" and not to enter these areas. At the Toxicology Unit of Medical Headquarters Croatia in Zagreb a spokesman for departmental head Professor Plavsic told me how they had been analysing soil, air and water samples smuggled out from these affected areas, leading to suspicion of use of chemical agents.

The pressure to use the full armoury of the most gruesome weapons of modern warfare would grow as winter set in. In eastern Slavonia it was still warm and sunny in October, an Indian summer of death. With the onset of colder, wetter weather and the likelihood of widespread snow the ardour for use of an unenthusiastic infantry was to diminish. Federal soldiers were still wearing their summer uniforms in October. The Croatians would soon be in a distinctly more comfortable position sitting it out in basements and cellars whilst their opponents shivered in the field.

Under fire, we aborted on our attempt to get up the road towards Vukovar from Vinkovci. Vukovar had already become the ikon of Croatian resistance and determination. On the radio they were singing sentimental songs about the ancient market town. On the walls there were posters. "Vukovar will never surrender". The toughest fighters - including many foreign mercenaries - were fighting in the rubble of the once prosperous centre. Thousands of inhabitants sheltered in cellars and basements from the constant bombardment. Civilians and soldiers alike died in the underground hospital, denied drugs and, even, anaesthetics. Some died of gangrene. Vukovar became Croatia's Stalingrad, physically and conceptually. But the bitter symbol of resistance was to fall around November 19 after 90 days of bloody siege involving sustained attack by tanks, heavy artillery, rockets, aircraft and, even, warships on the Danube. A myth of invincibility was smashed. The Hero City was no more. Either in the mind or in reality. There was just rubble left. But, out of the ashes and the rubble, another symbol - of martyred resistance - arose.

82

30 This woman seeks her missing husband at a prisoner reception centre in Zagreb.

31 Waiting for news of missing relatives, Zagreb, January.

32 The agony of waiting for news of relatives.

33 No news for this woman.

34 Lists of released prisoners of war are read out at the reception centre in Zagreb.

35 This man has just heard that his prisoner of war son has been released and is inside the centre.

36 Child refugees on the bridge at Pokupsko, September.

37 Young boy outside the presidential palace, Zagreb, August.

38 Bosnians flee by boat across the Sava, April.

39 Uncertain future. A young girl arrives by boat at Babena Greda, Croatia.

40 Refugees under fire flee across the bridge at Pokupsko.

41 For these young people the Yugoslav Federal Army is just a memory. Slovene youths celebrate in their old army uniforms in the streets of Ljubljana, March.

42 These young men have fled from Bosnia across the Sava at Babena Greda and are intercepted by Croatian soldiers: all men between 18 and 60 were returned to Bosnia for military service in the war.

43 Optimism in besieged Bosanski Brod.

44 Croatian military police dog unit, Djakovo, March.

As we drove out through the streets of Vinkovci they were deserted save for the odd soldier darting from doorway to doorway or loping across open spaces between shellbursts. On an impulse I asked my driver to stop when I noticed a large modern 'Pik' supermarket which had been shattered by shellfire. As I got out and raised the camera, a shell dropped into the middle of the road about a hundred metres ahead. Too close for comfort.

We fled from Vinkovci, without sampling the delights of the local hotel courtesy of American Express, the noise of the bombardment reverberating all around. Yet less than a kilometre away on the western outskirts of the town all was bafflingly normal. I could hardly believe my own eyes. A woman impassively pegged out her washing in the back garden of a neat detached house. Her husband was washing the car out front. And, in the distance, the plumes of smoke from exploding shells were clearly visible. The ability and determination of ordinary people to carry on normal life was quite baffling. It was almost as if they felt that by so acting they could somehow bring the tide of human events to a halt. Or it was maybe simply some sort of extreme display of the territorial imperative; a defiant last stand; a simple refusal to abandon the nest; or an inability to accept that such things could happen on your very own doorstep. I suppose that for most people - anywhere - home is the metaphorical womb, that most secure of places.

Things were very much the same in the town of Karlovac at Christmas, I was to find. Although the town was shelled every night; sporadically mortared during the day and the sound of machine-gun fire audible virtually all of the day and all of the night, after three months of this treatment people carried on much as normal. I wasn't sure at the time whether to put this down to human resilience or an inability to accept the inevitability of appalling events until they impinge absolutely.

Something war correspondent Martha Gellhorn wrote about the Spanish Civil War came to mind. "I decided that, these days, people would be well advised to love nothing. (Shorty) seemed to have arranged in her mind that the war was not coming here . . . no harm could strike this city; no evil could befall." [1]

Even then it was plain that whatever the winter might bring, one thing was certain. The course of the war would not be determined by the fate of Dubrovnik and its sadly shattered heritage, but in the beleagured towns and in the killing fields of eastern Slavonia.

Much nearer to Zagreb, on that road back from the front, we spotted some movement in the forest at the side of the road. We stopped the car and took a track into the forest, holding our hands aloft and announcing our arrival with shouted greetings. There were at least a dozen tanks that we could see dug in. That seemed to even up the odds a bit for the Croatians in the battering we had seen them taking. Then I noticed all the tanks had girls' names painted on them, the nearest one was 'Suzy'. Not a conspicuously Croatian name. Incredibly, these were American tanks - Shermans - dating, the commander told us, from 1936: captured from the local Federal army barracks. And most probably unused since the day they were built. That certainly didn't even up the odds quite so much.

Nevertheless, although we did not know it at the time, the tide was already turning. A modern army, established almost half a century previously, and of some 200,000 men with a modern armoury of weaponry, air and naval power, had ground to a halt in the face of an inifinitely smaller six month-old force of committed but, nevertheless, essentially untrained volunteers armed only with light weapons and whatever they had managed to capture from abandoned JNA facilities. In military terms, this failure was inexplicable. But, like so many armies before it, the JNA was in great measure defeated at home: by galloping inflation; shortage of foreign exchange; the printing of money and by an ever increasing lack of a public commitment to a continued conflict expensive in human as well as in financial terms. Add to this the foot soldier's positive disinclination to fight and the die was cast. So many Croatian soldiers I had met over the previous months had clasped their hands to their chests and declared, "But we have heart." It had seemed a fair propaganda point at the time but I had truly doubted its effectiveness as a military strategy. Ultimately, they were right. What an American journalist friend - Sherry Ricchiardi - had called "the rag tag army who have traded plows for guns, schoolbooks for grenades" actually turned the tide of war against all the odds.

Over that winter of war I got to know the long, tortuous road back to Zagreb from the eastern front rather well. I suppose I must have covered it all of twenty times and the passage along it was a sort of barometer of the progress of the war itself. During the autumn, in the dying days of the desperate defence of Vukovar, it was solid with war transport: with tankers full of fuel; lorries full of munitions; APCs, ambulances and captured JNA trucks bearing volunteers to the front. By December, the subtle pattern of transport on the road had changed: longer term supplies in container trucks for beleagured Osijek and Vinkovci; the German and Austrian lorries and vans with Caritas supplies and privately organised humanitarian contributions.

Just a few days before Christmas I covered that road - which normally took almost four hours to the front - in a little over two and a half hours at terrifying breakneck speed in an EC convoy taking the Croatian and JNA generals, Agotic and Rashita, to Osijek for peace talks. Escorted by Croatian special forces in black BMWs with their blue and red flashing rooflights, I pushed my little Citroen AX rental car to its very limits to keep up with the madcap dash to the shattered town. That was certainly the most instantly memorable journey down that road.

But there was, inevitably, always something new or remarkable on that long and winding road with its checkpoints - increasingly frequent as you neared the front - and its almost tangible quality of the exposed umbilical cord. There was a visit to the refugee centre at Podravska Slatina as a Caritas lorry drew up. "Oh no, not another delivery of food from Germany. Can't someone tell them that we have more food than we can eat around here?" The requirement, in fact, was for shoes and blankets.

Or there was the Ivan Dvor Lippizaner stud farm near Djakovo at Christmas. You could hear the rumble of heavy artillery fire just 20 km. or so from the frontline as the proud white Lippizaner horses pawed the the dirt floor of their stables and whinnied in terror. They have bred Lippizaners for the famed Austrian riding school in Vienna at Ivan Dvor since 1506. The best of the stock had already been evacuated to Hungary and to Lipica in Slovenia when I arrived but there was still, I reckoned, around two million pounds worth of stock left: a good Lippizaner of fine pedigree can be worth up to £150,000.

At Ivan Dvor there were two grooms left and a Croatian National Guardsman - Ilija Mariocenevic - and his seven year-old son Budimir. Even Budimir shouldered an AK-47 like a professional. "We remain here to the end to defend the horses."

But there was something which made a particularly deep impression on me on that road back to Zagreb from the frontline. During the early autumn of war in Croatia I had noticed several houses destroyed on the outskirts of the village of Suhopolje, not far from the town of Virovitica. They were modern, detached houses standing in their own once neat gardens. Now they were shattered beyond repair. On the road to the frontline, where houses destroyed by MIGS, rockets and howitzer shells had quickly come to constitute peculiarly unremarkable landmarks in the landscape of war, there was something quite strange about one of those houses, its front elevation completely gone and its roof blown away. I must have passed several times before I realised what it was.

There was a picture hanging on the wall. A photograph of a young boy left hanging there, amidst the confusion of the debris of the bedroom. It intrigued me for some reason I failed to rationalise, every time the car flashed by to or from the front. Something nagged at the back of my mind. It wasn't until the following spring when I pulled up the car one beautiful sunny morning, with a few minutes to spare on the four hour journey back to Zagreb, that I learned from a neighbour what was so different about the house at 28, Vuka Karadzica.

86

What was left of the contents appeared to have been selectively salvaged. I suppose I should have been more curious that a family shelled or bombed out from its house should abandon, of all things, the portrait of a beloved son. As I focused the long lens, I could read the inscription below the sepia photograph in Serbo-Croat: SKOLSKA USPOMENA. 'Souvenir of School'. He was a neat, intelligent looking boy of perhaps sixteen years, his arms folded above an open book. The picture suggested he was a scholar, a boy who loved his books. He looked ahead - confidently to a future of which he then must have had no inkling. The shattered mirror of his dressing table and his broken bed, piled high with debris, lay crushed below the strangely haunting image of hope and confidence.

There used to be a rather facile question on a long running BBC radio programme about three things you might salvage from your home as it went up in flames: frontrunners in this impertinent through-the-keyhole exercise were always dad's war medals, the family Bible or a prized family photograph. The small things it was supposed you might desperately salvage in the confused heat of flight. Even by such rough and ready criteria, something was surely wrong here.

As I stood at the side of the road poking the lens of the camera into the destruction of somebody else's world, focusing the 200mm. lens onto the enigma of that picture hanging on the wall amidst the ruins, an aged peasant dismounted from his old, black bicycle. He was weatherbeaten and wrinkled but he was smartly dressed. It was Sunday. He was returning from church. He stood and appraised me and, in turn, I looked him over. This could well have been his third war, I thought. He looked at the camera and seemed to understand what I was pondering.

"You know, we blew up this house with dynamite."

I was shaken. Shaken by the frankness of his admission. Shaken by the wanton destruction. And that in a country where randomly ruined houses hardly merited a second look. The house-damaged-by-rockets or Migs caption, which - even then - I had mentally written, was mentally spiked. This was different.

"When the three sons and the father of this house - they were Serbs, you see - went into the forest to join the Chetniks we drove out their mother and blew up their home."

Just like that. Then the aged Croat added after a moment's thought, quite matter of fact.

"There's a lot of that sort of thing going on these days."

And he got back on his bicycle and rode away.

The term "ethnic cleansing" came widely into use in the context of clearances by Serbs of Muslims and Croats from Bosnia from April 1992 onwards. This was clearly an earlier and less dramatic example of much the same phenomenon.

6. WAR ON THE INNOCENTS

So many of the descriptive images in the war for Croatia have been drawn from the Second World War. The besieged, battered and, ultimately, destroyed city of Vukovar became Croatia's Stalingrad. After the fall of Vukovar, Osijek became Croatia's Warsaw: waiting in fear to be overrun by an advancing army, victim of fate while the world watched. And in Zagreb, at a hospital for children, I found myself recalling the words of *The Times* correspondent when he reached Belsen in 1945. "It is my duty to describe something beyond the imagination of mankind."

The analogies with the Second War are not, I think, just because of a paucity of conceptualisation or expression. It is rather that in the 20th century that war has, until now, been synonymous with evil and suffering. Maybe Croatia will spawn its own powerful vocabulary and associated imagery. It is all too easy for war - any war - to become imbued with a romance; a quality of fantasy which all too conveniently ignores the very harsh realities. There are antidotes to this available. My own was a day at the Institute for Mothers and Children in Zagreb.

This is the hospital to which the most seriously injured children are brought from the front line of the war. There is no good time to be in hospital - either as patient or visitor. And this was one of the worst ones to be in, speaking just as a visitor.

There lie - in the wards and on the operating tables - the bleeding bodies of the truly innocent victims of a war without winners. There you can see the appalling damage which is inflicted by modern weapons of war on young, fragile bodies: a 12-year-old with his genitals torn away by shrapnel; a nine-year-old with shell fragments lodged in his brain, and others without arms or legs, some covered in terrible burns.

89

The surgeon in charge of efforts to try and save these torn and battered innocents is Dr Ivan Fattorini, a middle aged doctor with a warm but businesslike manner. Three years of his paedeatric training was carried out at Edinburgh's Royal Infirmary and at the same city's Western General Hospital. When I told him I was from Edinburgh, he beamed - quite the only time in our meeting. "I have fond memories of my time in Scotland. Please take back to the people there the true story of the horror of this war."

With that, I was handed a green surgical gown, face mask and plastic overshoes. Then we went into the operating theatre for an experience I have no desire to repeat.

For one terrible morning, I tried as best I could to cut my mind off from the physical horrors of terrible injuries. I busied myself with taking photographs and making notes, conscious of an awesome sense of responsibility: an obligation to communicate and to convey what I was seeing.

The first victim in the operating theatre was nine-year-old Goran from Vinkovci. This pretty city, with its 19th century buildings, lies to the south-west of now notorious Vukovar. In one of the many indiscriminate attacks launched long distance style by the armoured legions of the Serbian led Federal army, Goran had a substantial part of one calf and the flesh from one foot torn away by shrapnel from the explosion of a shell, as he ran for shelter as fast as his young legs could carry him. Now he faces many long and painful years of surgery and skin grafts.

Next in to the theatre, to have his wounds dressed under anaesthetic, was 13-year-old Aleksander from Pakrac, another town almost totally devastated by artillery and air bombardment. For months, the Chetniks pounded the town with mortars. The Federal army shelled it. The sound of snipers was to be heard almost every minute of daylight in the autumn of '91 when I visited. And, when the weather, was good, the Migs swooped down with rockets, bombs and machine cannon.

Aleksander was in the street during a bombardment when an artillery shell exploded near to him. His body was covered by shrapnel wounds. Shrapnel does not cause neat incisions. It gouges out large lums of flesh, often exposing arm and leg bones, which are also damaged. Tiny fragments lodge deep in the body and the surgeons work like detectives to uncover the trail of destruction. Where shrapnel, or modern bullets, leave the body there are hideous, gaping exit wounds.

Such was the state of young Aleksander's body. From time to time, as the team of doctors and nurses worked over him, the small eyelids would flutter open, unseeing, and the anaethsetist would adjust a drip.

I wanted to leave this hell. To pretend that such things do not happen to children in the last decade of the 20th century. But I could not turn my back on the scene before me just to appease my own feelings of sickness and unease. I was, however, glad to be ushered eventually from the theatre.

If I thought my vision of hell was over I was mistaken. In the intensive care wards the bedsheets were pulled back to show young boys with the most terrible of injuries - injuries I would never have believed any child could survive. Another boy from Vinkovci had tiny fragments of metal - flying shrapnel - lodged in his brain. He lay quite still. Prostrate in his bed unable to speak or to move. All control of his small body was gone, except for the eyelids which continued to flutter. Whether he saw or not, nobody - not even the doctors - knew. One explained, "This boy needs the most specialist of treatment and we can do no more for him here."

A special hospital in Marseilles had agreed to take him and, even, to send a plane. But the Federal authorities in Belgrade had long since closed Zagreb airport to all traffic and refused to open it - even for such a mission of mercy.

The misery of most of these wounded innocents was made all the worse by the fact that the towns and villages from which they came had either been razed to the ground or surrounded by the forces of the Chetniks and Federal army. As a result, they were cut off from their mothers and fathers and all their relatives. They had no visitors. For them, there were no cheering telephone conversations to home. No family comfort. No hospital visits. Not only did the children not know anything of their parents but their mothers and fathers - if indeed they were still alive - were living far away with no news of their injured children taken so abruptly to hospital from the battlefield.

The medical staff, like doctors and nurses all over, had every appearance of dedication and resourcefulness. They had ensured that every child had one toy. Some wards had television. But the TV channel in Zagreb broadcast virtually nothing but constant war reports, documentaries and stiff-upper-lip propaganada. There are seemingly endless images of dead bodies, soldiers firing weapons and shattered buildings. Then onto the flickering screen comes a column of soldiers filmed in soft focus making their way through the verdant forests and fields in the light of early morning to the strains of Dire Straits' *Brothers in Arms*. Hardly fit fodder for young minds so recently and bitterly caught up in the reality of war.

In other wards, I saw children with serious or long term illnesses. All these children were similarly cut off from their parents and relatives. Some could, in fact, have left hospital but there was simply no-one to take them home. And so they lay in bed day after day, bored and listless. For many of them I was their first visitor for a very long time. A couple of the little faces registered interest. One even smiled. I felt inexplicably embarrassed and self-conscious.

Those suffering from various forms of cancer were threatened with death. Not because they could not be saved but because of a chronic short of drugs with which to continue tumour treatment. Croatia was cut off from central banking functions which had operated from Belgrade - and the facility to get any convertible foreign currency. It was simply not possible to buy further supplies or, indeed, to fly in temperature sensitive hospital drugs.

92

In a cot in the corner was four-year-old Alen. Dr Mladen Cepulic took down the side of the cot from which Alen stared out impassively. On the white sheet beside him was a menacing black shape. I recoiled automatically at the image. In fact, it was just a toy: a life-sized toy machine gun, but accurately moulded from hard plastic.

There was no smile on his face as he grasped for his own personal weapon in the face of an intruder he did not recognise. I could not stop myself from drawing back momentarily.

"We have tried to give him a cuddly toy," Dr Cepulic explained apologetically, "But all he wants is his gun."

Such are the seeds which have already been sown in the next generation of war torn Croatia. Outside in the streets the children are playing a local version of Cowboys and Indians: National Guardsmen v. Chetniks. None of the children want to be on the side of the 'baddies'. Some of the children are kitted out in junior versions of the camouflaged combat fatigues worn by their fathers and older brothers, quite probably fighting less than an hour's drive from the capital.

You hardly need to be a child psychologist to hazard a guess at the long term effects. Zarko Korac of Belgrade University is, and he is in no doubt about the effects. "Parents are so obsessed by the war that there is a narrowing of the fields of interest. Parents are serious. They are confused and there is a high level of aggression - an aggression they themselves are not aware of. This is narrowing the horizons of children, providing a gap in their growth, a lack of fun and other focuses of interest."

The atavistic, ethnic hatreds are perpetuated. "Ours is a Homeric society - stories are passed from generation to generation. The hatred of Serb for Croat, of Croat for Serb, the militarism and glorification of war heroes is taking our society backwards, to a tribal level."[1]

I went from the hospital out into the welcome cold, fresh air of the Zagreb autumn, the streets busy with the normalcy of shoppers and office workers, struggling to cope with the things I had seen. Trying to absorb and to rationalise them. But I could find no solution to my own confusion.

On December 18 1991 Paul Harris returned to The Institute for Mothers and Children in Zagreb with 40 kgs. of cytostatic cancer drugs donated by Cyanamid, Bayer, Eli Lilley and Pharmitalia.

7. KILLING THE MESSENGER

Nineteen hundred and ninety-one was a bad year for journalists. Especially journalists in Yugoslavia. On December 30 the Brussels-based International Federation of Journalists announced that it had been the worst year ever for the deaths of journalists covering the world's conflicts. A total of 83 had died: and the day the figures were announced a Worldwide Television News cameraman died in the frontline Croatian village of Turanj, just outside Karlovac.

The journalist who died was Zivko Krsticevic. I met him a week before he died: we both pursued the EC convoy from Zagreb to Osijek which conveyed the Serbian and Croatian Generals Rashita and Agotic for more than 300km. at breakneck speeds across Croatia. Every so often, Zivko would thrust his bulk through the roof of the WTN Mazda to film the long speeding convoy of EC and official cars. It made a dramatic image as we sped through the dark countryside under the escort of Croatian special forces units in their black Seven series BMWs, their blue and red lights flashing in the night. It is one of those strange facts of life that you make friends quickly in war. A great bear of a bearded man I took to him immediately: he was accepting and fun, apparently fearless and determined to get the best pictures.

That night we went to the only surviving restaurant in Osijek. Snow was falling and we were all exhausted by the difficult dash across Croatia - and very hungry. We were refused entry because the EC monitors and the Generals had blockbooked the restaurant. Zivko just brushed the armed guards aside with an enormous grin and the rest of us followed in his wake.

Over dinner we joked about the risks: the pros and cons of sitting next to the window were examined in some detail. Then we were joined by a French photographer from the Sigma

95

agency, Antoine Gyori. He had been in Croatia since September and had the reputation of the cat with the proverbial nine lives. At the beginning of October he was in Karlovac in a bar with the Canadian freelance photographer Peter Brysky and a group of Croatian Guardsman when they came under mortar fire. Only Antoine survived. On another occasion his car came under machine gun fire and his travelling companion was hit.

I was wearing an ex-Gulf War NATO flak jacket which occasioned some amused banter. I asked Zivko, who was travelling with crew members Masa and Igor, if they wore flakjackets. Masa said they carried just one in the car. "In the morning we toss a coin to see who will wear it today." We all laughed but later, after his death, when I read Zivko's own notes, I became aware of the mental turmoil his work brought. "You're filming a friend while doctors fight to save his life. That really affects you deeply. Not when you're shooting it but when you get home. You accumulate these emotions and when you start to think about it all it can be really burdening."

The imperative of covering the war from the frontline is clear from Zivko's testimony. WTN is, necessarily, a competitive news gathering agency selling its footage on the open market. The best pictures are where the fighting is closest and so he took the risks, going right up to the frontline. "You put your life into a Guardsman's hands. He takes you the safest way . . . But let me tell you a story about when a Guardsman took us to the village of Barilovic, along the Kupa river, and it was just 50 metres away from the Chetniks. We were not aware of that until we entered Barilovic. Only then did we realise how dangerous it was because nobody was there, not a single soul. By the expression on the Guardsman's face, I realised we were in a very dangerous situation. We found the way out and ran away."

Other times it was not so much simply to get the pictures but a response to a challenge. A primitive game. "Sometimes you are provoked by the Guardsmen. They ask you 'Do you really have the guts to go to the frontline with us?' And then I answer 'Why not? If you go, why shouldn't I go with you?' And then it is

96

often even more dangerous than usual, just because they want to check you out."

At that point there is no fear but "there's always a moment when you're scared, scared you will get killed but the most difficult moment comes afterwards when I have seen all those difficult things, all those destinies of other people . . . you cannot experience it on the TV screen, not even 15 or 20%, compared to the real feeling of being there, shooting peoples' emotions in order to bring home the disasters of war as accurately as possible."

Zivko died of shrapnel wounds to the legs and chest after a mortar exploded beside him near the bridge at Turanj. He was dead before he reached the hospital in Karlovac. He left his camera running as he died. Two other journalists with him - Bruno Moser from Swiss Teletext and Stephan Kloss from *Sachsiche Zeitung* - were wounded in the same explosion. It was the foreigners' first trip to a war zone in Croatia.

Zivko was experienced. He shot his first footage at the Marshall Tito Barracks at the beginning of June as the tanks left to attack neighbouring Slovenia. Ordinary citizens tried to stop the tanks; Molotov cocktails were thrown and a young man was killed. The tanks were not halted but this was first manifestation of physical opposition by Croatians and it was captured on videotape. Zivko worked all over Croatia but especially in the area around Karlovac, Duga Resa and Turanj.

From his own notes and testimony, it would seem that Turanj, where he was to die, exercised a strange and, ultimately, fatal attraction. "Turanj was interesting to me because there are two bridges between Turanj and Karlovac, two rivers separating these two places. We all know the meaning of the word bridge. It joins together or separates something. In this particular case, it joins as well as separates. Everything happens at that bridge. People, refugees running away from the Chetniks; the army crossing it to get to the other side; people fight in Turanj; people get killed in Turanj, the wounded come back; the dead are brought back; ambulances rush there. In Turanj, on that bridge, there is all of war and life happening." Before his death, he was well aware of the risks at Turanj. "In Turanj you never know where the sniper is waiting for you. Sometimes it looks really quiet, and yet it may be at its most dangerous, because when the shells fall you hide somewhere but with the sniper one deadly shot is enough." In the event it was the mortar shell.

A quarter of the worldwide deaths among journalists in 1991 occurred in the Croatian conflict. Meantime, over that same tragic New Year that Zivko died, a question mark hung over the fate of another journalist. In a hotel room in Zagreb a young woman and a seven-year-old boy lived out the long days in a lonely limbo unable to accept the possibility that a husband and a father might never return. There were, of course, many thousands of people throughout war torn Croatia who anxiously awaited news of relatives that Christmas and New Year. So many had disappeared from sight in the turmoil and confusion of a country with then around three quarters of a million refugees and an official death toll pushing up towards the 10,000 mark.

But 31-year-old Sinisa Glavasevic disappeared not because he was taken in battle as a soldier or dispossessed of his home as a refugee. On November 19 he had been physically abducted - kidnapped, not to put too fine a point on it - by Serbian soldiers from the hospital convoy leaving defeated Vukovar. His crime, in Serbian eyes, was very real. He was a successful and respected radio journalist with Radio Vukovar who had consistently, over the months, brought reports of the beleagured town to listeners in Croatia and beyond. Nothing has ever been heard of him since.

His wife Majda, at 29, would probably accord neatly with most British preconceptions of the Balkan woman: thick black hair, dark of complexion and with what, in happier circumstances, might be termed laughing eyes. She has a wild gipsy-like beauty but there is nothing undisciplined about her manners or bearing. Neat and graceful, notwithstanding her awful predicament, she bears a heavy load with a dignity and forbearance which belies her years.

98

Sinisa and Majda married eight years ago in Vukovar, her husband's home town on the banks of the Danube in the eastern part of Croatia known as Slavonia. At that time Vukovar, now as much an icon for total devastation as Stalingrad, was an ancient and beautiful city with its stately Baroque buildings and its relics of the Austro-Hungarian empire. A year later, their son Bojan was born and, as is common in Croatia, the family went to live with Sinisa's parents and, over a period of several years, built on an extra floor to their house as a home.

Two years ago Sinisa joined Radio Vukovar, the local radio station, as a reporter and at the beginning of this year was promoted to producer position. "A year ago it seemed we had everything." Majda tells how he was successful at his work and with the outbreak of war in Croatia in July, he threw himself into the reporting of the attacks on his city with that vigour and determination to 'tell the story' which marks out the dedicated journalist. "He loved his work and was determined to carry on with it despite all the dangers. No matter how heavy the shelling he would always go out and bring back his reports from the shelters and the frontlines."

With sadness in her heart, Majda resolved to leave Vukovar with Bojan at the beginning of August and they travelled to the then comparative sanctuary of her parents' house in Bosnia. She placed no pressure on her husband to leave with her. "He was devoted to his work and for him it was something he simply had to do. I could not make him go against that." At the beginning of September they were reunited for a few hours at the border between Bosnia and Croatia but, after that, their only communication was by telephone - Majda usually spoke to him on the line from Croatian radio headquarters after his nightly radio broadcast updating Croatia - and the world - on the fate of Vukovar.

"We last spoke on the evening of November 8". Majda remembers dates she must have gone over in her own mind hundreds of times without a hint of hesitation. "He told me that negotiations were going on with the Serbian army and he was hopeful everything would be OK".

The next day he went out into the town to visit army headquarters and people in the shelters and came under fierce mortar fire. Wounded in the face, he was rushed to the underground hospital at Vukovar - from which he continued to report after just a few days, despite his injuries. With the fall of the city, it was agreed by the army with the International Committe of the Red Cross that all the patients from the hospital be evacuated to hospitals in Serbia. The evacuation was started before the ICRC arrived and, according to the statements of doctors and other patients, Sinisa was forcibly taken from the convoy as it left the town. Also taken were his two travelling companions who had come to look after him en route: his father and grandmother.

Nothing has been heard of any of them since. Most disturbingly, the Federal army authorities were soon flatly denying ever having siezed him and enquiries from the ICRC, Amnesty International and the International Federation of Journalists were ignored in Belgrade. Information given at the Foreign Press Bureau in Zagreb in December baldly stated: "He is suspected to have been executed by the Yugoslav army."

You could see why they were not sanguine at the Press Bureau. When you register there you can take away a closely typed six-page dossier entitled *The War in Croatia: Reported Attacks on Journalists*. This details more than 50 attacks by Serbians and Chetniks on journalists covering the war. By the end of 1991, 18 were positively confirmed as having died and a further three had been missing since September 3 and were assumed to be dead. The death toll of journalists in Croatia was now statistically greater in just six months than in the Vietnam war, or any other conflict since the Second World War.

The death of her husband was not a scenario which Majda could contemplate. "I cannot accept in my mind the situation where Sinisa does not come back to us." It was difficult for her to stay brave. Her eyelids were puffed and swollen and as we talk her eyes moisten and the tears roll down her cheeks. "I remember the beautiful things from our past together and just look to the future - to better times."

100

45 Six year-old Budimir Mariocenevic at Ivan Dvor Lippizaner stud farm.

46 Lippizaner horses at the Ivan Dvor stud farm, near Djakovo, eastern Croatia.

47 Sixty year-old Rozika Militic, grandmother and tank commander *extraordinaire* from the village of Kamenica.

48 Snjezana ('Snow White') Paradzikovic from Semeljci in eastern Croatia. She joined the Croatian National Guard when the Serbs shelled her village.

49 After almost a year of war, crops rot in the fields near Vinkovci, May.

50 "Everything is gone." Peasant woman at Plostice, on the road to Pakrac.

Majda knew then that their home in Vukovar had been destroyed, the contents looted and that she had nothing in the way of possessions left. Not that they would have been of any importance to her. The return of Sinisa was all she longed for.

As we talk, Bojan shifts restlessly, but politely, in his seat. Bojan does not yet understand the situation. He is a bright and irrepressible bundle of energy dashing here and there. He is learning English from the journalists who stay in the same hotel and a photographer has given him a a one-use camera which he carries around his neck at all the interviews he is now becoming so adept at handling. And he talks all the time of what they will do together when daddy comes home.

Majda and Bojan had a lousy Christmas in their hotel room. There was no Christmas tree, no decorations. "We decided we did not want to celebrate this Christmas. It was too sad to even be with our relations so, for us, it was just as a normal day". The only concession to the occasion was when they watched Mass from the Vatican together. Then the television with its feast of carols and entertainment was firmly switched off by Majda.

As we talk, it is abundantly clear that Majda does not look for sympathy - although she would like to think that others might bring as much pressure as possible to bear on the Serbians to respond to the requests for information. Her innate dignity does not allow her the indulgence of self-pity. There is just an awful lot of fatalism about her sadness. "At the moment there is just an empty space around. I don't wish to think of the worst. I can only look forward with optimism. But last year we had everything. This year we have nothing." As the New Year came, in that lonely hotel room, Majda Glavasevic offered up her prayers that 1992 might bring just one piece of news; that just one New Year wish might come true.

There is no happy ending to this story: no news of Sinisa or his fate. Attacks on journalists have continued and, by the end of August 1992, there were a recorded 32 deaths. In Sarajevo, most of the major news providers had suffered losses through injury, including CNN, ITN and the BBC's top war correspondent, Martin Bell.

8. BOSNIAN TINDERBOX

At the end of January of 1992 it was as if the landlocked
Yugoslav republic of Bosnia Herzegovina was physically under
siege. There was but one route by road to the north and to
Western Europe beyond - over the heavily defended iron bridge
into Croatia at Slavonski Samac. Over this bridge - reduced to a
single track by the controlling Croatian military - came
hundreds of lorries every day carrying goods from Bosnia; cars
taking Bosnians - and citizens of further flung republics from
what had constituted Yugoslavia - to visit relatives in Croatia;
coaches, campers and luxury cars transporting migrant workers
gastarbeiters - to their jobs in Germany; and, from time to time,
buses containing prisoners of war and refugees from Serbia
back to Croatia. Once over the bridge from Bosnia, through the
military control and into Croatia, traffic was directed into a
filling station: a filling station without petrol where the police
and customs checks were carried out beside the locked and
abandoned pumps.

All the other bridges into Croatia - with the sole exception of
the, then, pedestrian only route at nearby Slavonski Brod - were
either mined or blown up. Traffic to and from neighbouring
Serbia was reduced to a trickle at the border crossing point over
the Drina River at Zvornik. Oil and food no longer reached
Bosnia from Serbia and the queues were lengthening daily at
the filling stations. Air traffic into the capital Sarajevo was
severely curtailed and all access to the sea through Dubrovnik
and Ploce was now denied by the spread of fighting in
neighbouring Croatian territory.

The tension and paranoia within what has always been
regarded as the Balkan tinderbox of Bosnia was only too
evident in the ethnically and religiously divided republic. At the
roadblocks and checkpoints you were frequently unsure as to
exactly who was searching and interrogating you or, indeed,

why. Around Serbian areas Serbian police and irregulars manned the checkpoints; around Muslim areas there were Muslim volunteers; around traditional Croat areas there were Croatian Guardsmen; and in more mixed and strategic areas there were sometimes Bosnian territorials and sometimes Federal Army soldiers.

The first real clue as to who was emptying my bags, going through every last piece of camera equipment, my toiletries and currency only came when a black beret was triumphantly discovered at the bottom of the bag.

"What is this?" came the stern inquiry.

"It is a beret. It keeps my head warm in the cold - and dry when it rains." This statement of the obvious was clearly not appreciated and was returned with an accusation. "Are you in the Croatian army?" The hatred of the black beret - the trademark of the *ustase* in the Second World War - now marked my interrogator out as a Serb.

The explaining away of the black beret was relatively easy, even if it did provide a few sticky moments. Nagging away at the back of my mind all the while, however, was the NATO flak jacket underneath my coat on the back seat of the car. I sent up a short prayer that it would not be discovered - nor the Croatian Ministry of Information press pass lurking in my breast pocket and which I had hidden away as we crossed the bridge into Bosanski Samac. Once search and questioning was over, an animated roadside discussion developed amongst our interrogators as to what to do with us. One faction was in favour of sending us back over the border; another for further questioning and the more laid back for letting us carry on.

I played along with the pantomime and acted really stupid, looking them straight in the face with an inane grin. Ultimately, they decided we must be pretty harmless and waved us on. At the time my driver and I were on the road to Banja Luka: a large, modern city dominating a predominantly Serbian region. It was an important military centre, and, since the enforced withdrawal from Zagreb, headquarters of the Yugoslav army Fifth Command. As we drove into the city, arrayed on the runway of the military airport was a vast assortment of military hardware including assault helicopters and ground to ground missiles. Much of the armament evacuated by the Federal army from its bases in Slovenia and Croatia was now in Bosnia - ready fuel for the tinderbox.

In the centre of the city itself, at the Hotel Bosna, a six-strong UN delegation - from the total complement of 50 now in Yugoslavia - had established itself and was meeting with the military. The unexpected arrival of an unknown individual from the foreign press occasioned visible shock to the assembled security men. A courteous request to photograph the comings and goings produced a no nonsense response. "It is absolutely forbidden to take photographs of the United Nations," I was sternly advised by a stony faced, besuited denizen of the Serbian security service.

A request made directly to the UN personnel revealed more in the way of enthusiasm for a photo session but after a few pictures the police and military moved in. My papers, passport and press card, "were not in order." Evidently, in order to work in Banja Luka, it was necessary to travel to Sarajevo, register and collect papers: a good day's trip, if not two. The name or address of the bureau which had to be visited for granting of permission was not known - or, if it was, it was not being revealed. The studied bureaucratic obtuseness of these *apparatchiks* reminded me of the response of my Intourist guide in *pre-perestroika* Moscow when I asked to visit a prison. "We have no prisons. Crime is eradicated."

My besuited friend in Banja Luka hissed. "You leave town now." Adding menacingly, "Maybe we see you again." Definitely as much a threat as a promise.

Bosnia may not have been physically under siege but mentally its five million inhabitants seemed to be preparing for a conflict many saw as inevitable. Not only was the population split on ethnic lines - as in Croatia - with 31% Serbs and 17% Croatians,

104

but here 45% being Muslims introduced an additional and explosive religious dynamic. Just as the Croats looked to Zagreb for leadership and the Serbs to Belgrade, the Muslims were increasingly looking to Ankara, Tehran and Tripoli. Turkish Prime Minister Suliman Demirel had already made pointed comments about "our Turkish brothers in Bosnia" and Colonel Gadaffi had condemned the Serbs as "barbaric."

It seemed that, initially at least, Muslims and Catholic Croats would join together against the Orthodox Serbs in the coming conflict. There were appalling and unedifying precedents for such a course of action. In the last war, Muslims in the Foca region allied themselves with the Croatian *ustase*, forming the elite SS Handscher division and affixing the Nazi eagle emblem to the Turkish fez. At the end of the war, the Serbian *chetniks* took their terrible revenge: the Muslim Fascists were chained together in their thousands and thrown into the Drina where they drowned.

Half a century later, all sides were arming themselves against what even then was widely regarded as an inevitable conflict and one which would make the war in Croatia seem like a mere dress rehearsal. A referendum on independence for Bosnia was announced at the end of January but, even at that stage, it was thought that it would probably prove inconclusive as the Serbs immediately stated their intention to boycott it. Some Croats said that, rather than independence, they wished their territory to be joined to that of the independent Republic of Croatia. Radovan Karadzic, leader of the Serbian SDS Party, wanted a loose confederation of those republics left in what was Yugoslavia. This, in turn, conflicted with Belgrade's desire for Bosnia as part of a Greater Serbia. Meantime, Serbs in Bosnia had already declared no less than seven 'autonomous' regions within the republic.

The Muslims, for their part, harboured fears of dirty dealing between Belgrade and Zagreb. There were already allegations that, in return for Serbia's ceding occupied territory in eastern Croatia, it would give up historic claims on territory occupied by Serbs in Bosnia and would annexe distinctly Croatian areas.

105

This scenario could leave the Muslims in an embattled rump around Sarajevo. Even Karadzic was deeply unhappy at this prospect of division. "Enough is enough. We will defend ourselves. We will not allow the destruction of our homeland."

As I munched my way through the traditional delicacy of *cevapcici* - pastry and sausage - at the cafe in Bosanski Samac the owner bewailed the position of herself and other Muslims. "We are caught between the Croatians and the Serbs. Soon their war will be ours."

A lorry driver at another table nodded his agreement. Also a Muslim, from Sarajevo, the Croatian police had just stopped his lorry on the other side of the border. Its cargo of toys from Italy had been destined for Belgrade. But, he was told, it was illegal to carry goods across Croatia for the enemy in Serbia. And now he was without his lorry or its contents. An ominous portent for the future of beleagured Bosnia.

Ten days later somebody - Serb or Croat nobody knows for sure - went out at night and affixed plastic explosives to the central pier of the bridge at Slavonski Samac. A short time later they were detonated and the last road link between Croatia and Bosnia was closed for the meantime. The bridge was reopened on a restricted basis - one vehicle at a time being allowed to cross - but during the third week of April the fighting which was to escalate throughout Bosnia again closed the bridge as Bosanski Samac was taken by Serbian irregular forces. Muslim police in the town were killed and, even, it was reported, Muslim doctors in the hospital. The federal army then started to shell Slavonski Samac on the Croatian side of the river. That link had now become irrelevant.

At the end of February, just as United Nations peacekeeping forces prepared to move into Croatia, the conflict entered a new and even more dangerous phase with the physical explosion of tensions in the republic of Bosnia Herzogovina during the weekend of the referendum on independence.

It has been shown, time and again, in the volatile Balkans, that it only needs just one small spark to light the fuse. It came in Bosnia with the death of an unknown Serb - Nikolo Gardovica - at a Serbian wedding in the capital of Sarajevo. He was killed, allegedly, by "Croatian drug addicts" (in fact, two Croatians and a Muslim) - in terms reminiscent of a Reichstag style frame-up - as the referendum came to a close on March 1. His death brought masked Serbian gunmen onto the streets in what appeared to be an altogether rather too well rehearsed 'spontaneous' reaction.

When the Serbs dismantled the Sarajevo roadblocks three days later, they did so only after the city's Muslims had taken to the streets in mass demonstrations. Two Muslims died at the roadblocks in a fusillade of bullets. Now all sides in this ethnically divided republic had their first martyrs: their *casus belli*.

When the Indian General Satis Nambiar arrived a week later in Croatia and in Bosnia, he had to come to terms with the inescapable fact that he was moving his proposed 14,000 men into position as peace*makers* rather than peace*keepers*. Only the previous weekend the advance party of some 60 UN liaison officers had been pushed to the limit monitoring the fast changing situation in both Bosnia and neighbouring Croatia. In Croatia, just a few miles across the border with Bosnia, the white jeeps with their blue flags crisscrossed the empty roads which cut through the flat, abandoned farmland of eastern Slavonia as the UN men desperately tried to get warring Serbs and Croats to talk on their newly installed telephone 'hotlines'. But the Serbians were simply not taking calls as they rained rockets and shells onto the Croatian frontline towns and villages. According to the crisis centre in Vinkovci, there were 300 hits on the town - killing five people - and it was estimated that more than 500 shells fell on nearby Osijek.

The 15th ceasefire, which had theoretically been in force since January 3, had quite clearly irrevocably broken down: the

Bosnian referendum and its associated tensions, the much improved weather and general impatience were all playing their part. The Australian chief of the UN team, Colonel John Wilson, admitted at a press conference in Zagreb that weekend to being "very disturbed at these serious ceasefire violations." The careful Wilson was well known for his measured understatement.

For the UN, the violent end to Bosnia's referendum and the following week's events were adding to the considerable logistic problems. Roadblocks manned by Serbian irregulars had gone up in the tense northern regions a full two days ahead of those in Sarajevo. The roadblocks were put up to discourage Croats and Muslims from getting to the polls but in the city of Banja Luka, for example, this effectively neutralised the UN team based there.

For most of that week large parts of northern Bosnia were, without warning, cut off completely. I found myself on March 1 in the border town of Bosanski Brod as local Serbs (just 33% of the population) declared it to be a "self-governing autonomous Serbian district." Within hours there were roadblocks on every road out of the town and, by Wednesday, they were mining the roads following a night of mortar fire: 60 shells fell on the town - from which side nobody seemed to know. Local Serbs claimed that they came over from Croatia whilst the Croats alleged the Serbian irregulars were shelling the town to spread terror. The only way out of Bosanski Brod was by foot over a bridge across the River Sava. I was grateful for it - as were the hundreds of distressed Croatians who, by the end of the week, were fleeing the continuing fighting in the town. Meantime, young Serbs with Kalashnikovs were leaving their homes in the villages around Bosanski Brod. This was, quite simply, a chilling replay of the events which had begun the fighting in Croatia the previous July.

Thus it was that the war in Bosnia first started in Bosanski Brod. As I sat at a pavement cafe in the sun that weekend watching the comings and goings at the bus station, the bustle of the market and the frenetic activity of the pavement money changers, little did I guess at what the town would look like when I was to return just seven weeks later.

It was already clear then that in a strife torn Bosnia the UN peacekeepers would become impotent. As so many of the military offensives on Croatia had been mounted from Bosnia, now that most of the Federal troops evacuated from their barracks in Slovenia and Croatia were based there, the UN was relying on being able to monitor the peace from the republic. It was anticipated that it might not be possible to enter the Serbian held enclaves from the Croatian front lines and so Bosnia was to be vital to monitors and peacekeepers to facilitate access. The UN had also made logistic plans to base all its operations in Yugoslavia in 'neutral' Sarajevo. Within six weeks the capital itself was to be consumed by fierce fighting and, by the end of April, General Nambiar was forced to take the decision to abandon it as his headquarters.

The seemingly inevitable spread of the strife in Bosnia threatened to fudge the border with Croatia. It seemed likely that the Croatian army would enter Bosnia to defend Croats there who would come under attack from Serbs. Locally, Croats and Muslims were allying themselves. The Serbian led Federal army could be reckoned, in turn, to ally itself with Serbian irregulars - as it did in Croatia - and you did not need to be a visionary to conclude that the whole dangerous cocktail could well then lead to a more general war conducted with scant regard to border limitations.

The referendum itself highlighted rather than eased ethnic tensions. The Serbs (31% of the total population) said they would stay away from the polls - and that is exactly what they did. Muslims (45%) and Croatians (17%) made a virtual 100% turnout. In the event, 63% of the population went to the polls and of those 99.28% voted "Yes" for independence and the break with the Serbian/Montenegran rump of the old Yugoslavia. It was very hard to see how a bloody resolution could be avoided.

Originally, when the UN peacekeeping force for Yugoslavia was proposed, one of its principal *raisons d'etre* was to stop the spiral of violence before it reached Bosnia. That objective was now largely overtaken by events whilst, in Croatia, there was no longer much peace to keep. Military men there were hardening their attitudes and seemed increasingly inclined to push on with the war. As one senior officer put it to me, "You put the UN between us and the Serb positions and will never regain our lost territory. All those lives lost in places like Vukovar will be for nothing."

A fellow officer, somewhat the worse for wear, expressed the bravado and increased confidence which this volunteer army was now feeling. "Without the blue helmets between us, we could be in Belgrade by the summer." The opposition right wing Croatian Party of Rights and its military wing, HOS, was openly opposing the entry of UN troops. Its spokesman Mario Mihaljevic - "I am the, how you say, Dr Goebbels of our party" - told me unequivocally in Zagreb, "If UN troops try to stop us retaking the occupied territories we will have to kill them."

The tide of events in the Balkans can move with a terrifying speed, gathering its own relentless momentum. International response tends to grind equally slowly. It seemed distressingly likely that history would show that a combination of international lethargy and Balkan intransigence had led to a breakdown far beyond salvage by well meaning men of peace in blue helmets.

That breakdown was less than six weeks in the coming. Sarajevo - regarded as a model of ethnic tolerance and easy living - was paralysed by roadblocks, terrorised by Serbian snipers and gradually devastated by Federal army shellfire. Serbian irregular forces began to sieze territory throughout the republic from Zvornik and Bjelijna in the north to Mostar and Foca in the south. But Bosanski Brod was where it all started.

When I returned in the third week of April that cafe was burned out. The bus station was filled with gutted wrecks and there was not a single person to be seen on the street. The area around the cafe was now a free-fire zone between the Serbian and Bosnian forces and Bosanski Brod was a ghost town except for men in

110

uniform. When I had visited before it had been a prosperous town of some 35,000 people. Now, according to the vice-president of the Crisis Centre, just 4,000 remained. Virtually all of the population had fled under attack from heavy artillery, rockets and mortars which had rained down ceaselessly since the first week in March. Muslims and Croats were now indeed fighting side by side against a common enemy: the blue and white badges of the militia of an independent Bosnia alongside the green 'Allah is Great' badges of the Muslims.

Across the River Sava, Slavonski Brod also found itself under attack from the Serbs and now the 300 metre - long metal bridge was itself a free-fire zone providing a precarious link for food and military supplies for the beleagured defenders. Nevertheless, the artillery of the Federal army had failed to make a direct hit on the bridge, despite having destroyed the houses clustered around the Bosnian end. Serbian snipers were prone to fire randomly at anyone running the gauntlet over the bridge but now it was hardly used - apart from by military men and the odd journalist. The last remaining refugees preferred to make a safer crossing by boat at quieter spots.

At the Bosnian end of the bridge, Bosanski Brod was divided into two parts. As you drove into the town, the area to the left and straight ahead was held by the Serbs. You could not enter without invitiing the unwelcome attention of machine gun or mortar. A sharp right at the end of the bridge took you into the area controlled by Muslims and Croats, who had formed themselves into the lst Brod Bosnian Defence Brigade. Volunteers gathered in silent groups outside the Crisis Centre before being taken away to the front in a variety of lorries and vans. In the basement of the hotel along the road, a group of young volunteers set up, over the weekend of Easter, Radio Bosanski Brod, broadcasting news and information to the defenders on AM and FM with a tiny 300 watt transmitter.

The local fighters were all too obviously supplemented by men and arms from Croatia. Fighters from the right-wing HOS were much in evidence and a British mercenary from Vinkovci complained mightily to me a few days later that heavy artillery

111

and nightsight weaponry had been moved down from Croatia's eastern front to the besieged towns of northern Bosnia. Thus was the border, in practical terms, becoming meaningless and virtually unrecognisable.

This was not all. Both sides were effectively wearing the same uniforms. And so, that week in Bosanski Brod, Muslims and Croats wore pink ribbons dangling from their shoulders. At the Crisis Centre they admitted, "It's a bit confusing around here and so we've given out these ribbons for identification." When they ran out of ribbons, the soldiers wrapped pink toilet paper around their arms to protect themselves from their colleagues. In the heavy rain it rapidly became a sad and fragile protection.

Croats and Muslims were now surrounded in Bosanski Brod. The Serbians, for their part, had already declared their intention to create another Vukovar. The men there all seemed determined to fight to the end: and with their backs to the 300 metre wide river it seemed they might have little choice in practical terms.

On May 3 the bridge between Slavonski Brod and Bosanski Brod was attacked and seriously damaged by Federal warplanes, as the twin towns now came under attack from the air.

The fashionable young figure of Olga stood out in the huddle of black clothed peasant women scanning the Bosnian bank of the River Sava. Elegantly dressed in a colourful and stylish trouser suit, her patent leather shoes and white trousers were smeared by the mud of the riverbank and her rouged cheeks were streaked by tears. Otherwise, in a shopping plaza or discotheque in any European city the 24 year-old would have fitted into the stylish urban landscape, but, at a remote part of the border between Croatia and Bosnia, she cut an unlikely figure. The overall impression of unreality was increased by the deep rumbling sound of heavy artillery attacks a few miles away as Slavonski Samac, on the Croatian side of the border, came under attack. Olga's story reflected, in microcosm, the sudden and cataclysmic turn of events in Bosnia in the middle of April.

Like so many of her fellows, she worked in Germany - a *gastarbeiter* - earning prized Deutschmarks to supplement the meagre earnings of her peasant family in Bosnia. On Good Friday she arrived back for Easter. Just two hours after arriving back in her home village of Domaljevac she sat down with her family - her father, mother, two brothers and sister - for what was to be a happy, celebratory dinner of reunion. Then a Serbian neighbour entered the house and delivered an ultimatum: they must leave their home immediately, with none of their possessions, or face summary execution. The majority Croat population was to be cleared from the village which was now held to be Serbian territory. The women left, fleeing across the Sava in small boats: the men stayed to defend their territory with hunting rifles and knives.

For the dispossessed Muslim and Croat populations of Bosnia, war-torn neighbouring Croatia with its river border represented the only possible haven, yet virtually every connecting bridge had been destroyed. Necessity dictated that flight must, most often, now be by boat: small motor boats, barges and, even, rowing boats were, by the middle of April, carrying tens of thousands of Bosnians across the 300 yard wide rain swollen Sava at dozens of different locations. In the third week of April -seven weeks after the referendum on Bosnia's independence - around 3,000 women and children a day were arriving in small motor boats at a hastily improvised crossing point at Babena Greda. Here Olga came ashore, as bulldozers cleared a track through the fields down to the river and soldiers built up the landing stations. And it was here that Olga maintained her vigil, asking all the newly arrived for news of her village, her brothers and her father. None of these people carried more than a single pathetic bundle or, at most, a treasured bicycle. None of them had had more than a few minutes to gather together a few essentials. And they all shook their heads in response to Olga's questions.

The enormity of the tragedy enveloping Bosnia Herzogovena had yet to be appreciated by a world seemingly grown tired of the intractability of the Yugoslav problem. The latest breakdown and vicious war was vastly more complex, widespread and threatening to general European stability than the Slovenian or Croatian conflicts. In Bosnia, Catholic Croats, Orthodox Serbs and Muslims had lived together not just in the same villages and towns, but in the same streets and the same apartment blocks. Throughout the country an all encompassing process of division was now well advanced: Europe was already looking at not just a few thousand refugees but at one or, even, two million people on the move. Some Serbs were openly calling it a process of "ethnic cleansing" in terms disturbingly reminiscent of Hitler's drive for *lebensraum*. The clearing of villages, towns and, indeed, whole regions was taking place throughout the republic on a scale incomprehensible to anybody who had not witnessed something of it.

For two days that April I stood at a narrow wooden footbridge precariously supported by scaffolding over a deep gorge. The main bridge lay collapsed below - destroyed by the Croatians on November 15 as Federal tanks advanced. This bridge once connected the Bosnian town of Brcko to the Croatian village of Gunja. The narrow single-file walkway was now the only bridge link to safety for the refugees who stretched away on the other side as far as the eye could see. They crossed at the rate of 1,000 an hour from six in the morning to eleven at night: the thousands of women and children left on the other side at 11 p.m. simply stood patiently until the next morning when the bridge reopened. On the Saturday night it was bitterly cold and there were flurries of snow. God knows how they survived. As I counted them through over two days, I reckoned that, at this one small and necessarily limited crossing point, at least 15,000 people a day were fleeing to safety. This was symptomatic of a mass human exodus of vast proportions. When you added in the 10,000 a day who were crossing in iron barges nearby at Zupanja; the 3,000 a day by motor boat at Babena Greda and the thousands more at a dozen other crossing points, you soon come to the inescapable conclusion that around 100,000 women and children a day were crossing into Croatia.

The haste of their evacuation was all too apparent. Mothers often carried nothing but babes in arms. Nobody carried more than one bundle or a couple of plastic carrier bags. One small boy simply carried his pet goldfish in a plastic container, his last link with an ordered home he would certainly never know again. But what was most apparent was that this was a movement of women and children: there was not a single young or healthy man in the thirty thousand or so who passed in those two days.

Instead, a body of men built up on the Croatian side of the bridge and, two or three times every hour, the passage of the refugees was briefly stopped and hundreds of men were allowed over into Bosnia. When you talked to them you came to realise that these were men who, in their own way, were giving up as much as the refugees passing in the other direction. These were men who had been working in Germany, Austria, Switzerland, or wherever, as *gastarbeiters*. They had given up their jobs and were returning for one elemental reason: to fight for their homeland against the Serb aggressor.

The fight was not far away for them. Just over the bridge, the Serbs were starting to divide the town of Brcko. Its 50,000 population comprised just 20% Serbs but, nevertheless, large areas of it - including the oil refinery, food plants and Volkswagen battery factory - had been claimed as Serbian territory and, over the weekend of Easter, Federal army lorries dropped their tailboards in the Serbian districts and distributed guns to the population. The role of the Serbian dominated army at that local level was all too apparent to those on the ground.On a much wider level, Croatian officials had already come to the conclusion that the Serbs, having signally failed to crush Croatia in war, now intended to bring down the republic by crude and crushing economic means: by the introduction of more than a million, maybe as many as two million, refugees.

115

On the Croatian side of the border three soldiers policed the influx of refugees, lending an arm to the elderly, carrying a child for an exhausted mother or gathering up the spilled contents of plastic bags. Of the three, Ramis was a Muslim; Borislav a Serb; and Ivan a Croat: Their evident camaraderie puzzled me in the face of the violent events taking place just five minutes further down the road. Later that day, as the refugees poured past the windows of the local school hurriedly converted into a refugee centre, I asked the President of the Community of Gunja how could he rationalise this contradiction? It was an unfair question, of course because this was the question at the very root of the Yugoslav conflict; a question the answer to which - if there could only have been a sane and rational answer - would have provided the key to unlock the ethnic problems of the sick federation.

He shrugged his shoulders and looked immensely sad. "I think if the Federal army or the Chetniks come to Gunja then our Serbian friends will feel obliged to follow their historic roots. They will then no longer be our friends." There lay the whole tragic, atavistic inevitability of this Balkan conflict. And so it came to pass that Olga found herself thrown out of her home, another forlorn refugee on the banks of the Sava.

The bridge over the River Sava connecting Brcko and Gunja was blown up early in the morning of April 30. Masked men in camouflage uniforms siezed Croatian Guardsmen at the pedestrian bridge and set off explosive charges. It was packed with refugee women and children at the time: more than twenty were killed and many wounded.

It might have been a perfect summer's afternoon. The sun shone fiercely on the lush green fields which sloped down to the River Bosna. The poppies had bloomed throughout northern Bosnia and the blood-red flowers combined to make a brilliant patchwork quilt of rich red and green.

116

51 Shattered ambulance, Vidusevac, September.

53 Mass grave of Croatian volunteers who died fighting for Dubica at Tazan Church, September.

52 Mortar impact on the front of the church, Vidusevac.

54 House destroyed by a direct artillery hit in the old town of Karlovac, Christmas Eve.

55 'Ceasefire' damage at Zagrebacki Blok, Vinkovci, March.

56 The church at Toran.

57 Blasted Baroque. Direct artillery hit in the centre of Osijek.

58 Repairing the damage of war at Vinkovci, May.

59 Roses at the gate. A home destroyed in aerial attack, Odzak, northern Bosnia.

60 The bridge at Zupanja blown up to prevent JNA tanks crossing into Croatia.

Above the brown-tiled roofs of the villages in the valley, the narrow pencil shape of the tower of a mosque pokes through here; the onion dome of of a Serbian Orthodox church there; and the Baroque bell towers of the Catholic churches. To the right is the town of Modrica, shimmering in the midday heat, just a couple of kilometres below. But this summer idyll was a sham: a mirage.

Somewhere to the left there is the ear-splitting report of an outgoing shell. Maybe seven or eight seconds later there is a more distant explosion and a plume of smoke rises from the town. A chain reaction is seemingly prompted. Shells are fired from the left and and from the right and a cacophony of machine-gun fire starts from within the town.

Just as in Sarajevo, Modrica is in the process of being divided. At the end of May, the northern part was held by Serbian irregular forces, the south by Croats and Muslims bound together in fragile alliance. As in Sarajevo, they were fighting street by street for control of the town.

From outside, Croatian artillery and mortars bombarded the northern suburbs. The federal army and Serbian irregulars bombarded the Croats and the Muslims in the south. Electricity was cut off in much of the town and food supplies got in from time to time during lulls in the fighting. The Croatians with me say this was never a Serbian town. They say it was 80% populated by Croatians. This ethnic Croatian claim to the town was tangibly backed by soldiers from neighbouring Croatia.

I am told they are volunteers come to fight for freedom. The reality on the ground looks somewhat different. At a roadside cafe in the nearby town of Odzak soldiers newly arrived from Osijek in eastern Croatia are jumping down from a lorry and, a few days later, a boy from Djakovo tells me that he was simply ordered to report for duty. The border between Croatia and ethnically Croatian Bosnia is becoming blurred.

The road to Modrica from the border crossing at Bosanski Brod is maybe 60 kilometres. What traffic there is is mostly one way

117

towards Odzak and Modrica. There is little civilian traffic and, indeed, you get the feeling most of the population has fled the area. The jeeps, cars and trucks on the road are flying the Croatian flag as they head for the battle for Bosnia.

The journey from Bosanski Brod to Modrica provides some unedifying sights. The bridge at the border has been the object of many weeks of aerial attack. Although Mig 29s have blown holes the size of the average family car all along the bridge, they have, inexplicably, failed to destroy it. While I was staying a few hundred yards away, a helicopter gunship flew over the bridge and launched three missiles. They exploded ineffectively on the road leading to the bridge, leaving holes about 20 cm. deep. Two days later, a similar attack had more tragic consequences on the Croatian side when three children at play were killed on the pavement in Slavonski Brod.

To cross over the bridge, you manoeuvre the car around the holes and over the heavy steel sheeting which covers the largest. Just a few weeks previously, the Serbs held everything to the left of this bridge and, as you turned left, to Modrica, you can see that every single house is blown up or burnt out. Houses line the road in a litoral strip for maybe ten kilometres. Not one house stands fit for human habitation: maybe 400 or 500 houses lie ruined. You cannot look too hard at this panorama of destruction lest you lurch into the shell craters which pockmark the road. Some of the houses still smoulder, others are actually burning. The sides of the road are littered with dead animals. Here there is a blackened sheep, there a cow wedged into the ditch, its four legs stuck into the air in *rigor mortis* like some carelessly upturned table. As you drive past, the flies rise up in a great black cloud and the stench of decaying flesh mixes with the acrid smoke from the burning buildings. And, every so often, there is a burst of light machine-gun fire or the crack of a sniper. Then it's foot to the boards time.

There are checkpoints every few miles. Some are manned by youngsters in makeshift uniforms and trainers, others are strangely abandoned. Around a corner sits an uncompromising notice in the road: MINEN! A hundred metres ahead, a heavy

118

machine gun is mounted on a tripod facing directly at you - but no-one is positioned behind it. Decision time. To go ahead or not? I draw into the side of the road and wait for the next car to pass - maybe ten minutes later - and follow on past the abandoned military hardware.

After the town of Odzak, the road is littered with mines - by which side you know not but, then, that is somewhat academic. Tanks and armoured personnel carriers take to rough farm tracks and across fields, throwing up great clouds of dust as they race to join the battle for Modrica. I choose to climb to the top of a hill for a panoramic view and spend the afternoon watching the shelling of the town and its inhabitants. Like some sort of irregular ping pong game the shells are lobbed in from one side, then the other. At one point, a shell lands a couple of hundred metres ahead in the middle of a field. The Croatian soldiers laugh. "*Nashe.*" One of ours. This is "friendly fire."

On the road back, more houses are burning at the sides of the road. Something about this puzzles me. Then, on the outskirts of one village, I see a group of young men taking petrol canisters from the back of a trailer. They go to a house and jettison the liquid through the broken windows. The building is enveloped by flames.

I now realise what is happening. Croatians are burning the houses once occupied by Serbs who had now fled. History was, quite simply, repeating itself. Marshal Marmont, Napoleon's general and ruler of the Illyrian States which included Croatia, describes in his memoirs a certain penchant on the part of Croatian soldiers. He noted, on the constantly contested border between east and west, their enthusiasm for the burning of Bosnian villages. Of course, then they were burning Muslim villages in this 18th century manifestation of scorched earth warfare. Tried and tested measures are arguably the most effective. By this same bitter strategem two hundred years later, they seek to ensure that it is their Serbian neighbours who will never ever return. Quite likely those Serbs who have fled will never return, but in this quagmire of madness it seems more than likely that their sons or grandsons may return one day for

119

vengeance. And what of the one and a half million refugees already without homes? The destruction of perfectly sound property seems a peculiar insanity.

In a farmhouse kitchen in the village of Pecnik, just outside Modrica, I am served a plate of steaming goulash by the three generations of women of the house. The head of the household shakes his head sadly as the detonations resound all around. "I no longer know nor understand what is happening in my country. This is just a great madness."

120

9. RETURN FROM VUKOVAR

Off the convoy of buses they came - 270 of them - down into the bitterly cold January night, their eyes blinking in the glare of the TV lights. These were the men, and a few women, of Vukovar and some of the neighbouring villages returning to Croatia from the Serbian prison camps.

The uncompromising lights of the TV cameras reflected off the snow seemed to harshen the gaunt features and the hollow looks. Many of the men had shaven heads, some wore striped pyjamas. It was all disturbingly redolent of the images of another war I knew only from books and films. These civilians had spent some two months or more detained in Serbian camps. Now, in freedom, they were not exactly home with their arrival at Slavonski Samac, the only border crossing point in those days from Bosnia into Croatia. Where their homes used to be in eastern Slavonia there was now virtually total devastation and the towns and villages were held by Serbian forces. But, at the very least, they were released from the physical horrors of imprisonment.

Five hours later they stepped down from the buses outside a sports complex on the outskirts of Zagreb. They looked desperately around in the hope of seeing some friend or relative in the crowd beyond the TV lights. Occasionally, a shout would come from the crowd and a mother, brother or sister would rush forward for a joyous reunion. The leaner and hungrier looking prisoners were embraced by the microphones of TV and radio reporters. One man pulls up his shirt in the cold, raw night to show his rib cage a mass of bruises; another prostrates himself on the snow to demonstrate how he must sleep on his side on the stone floor in the confined space of the crowded camp. A smartly dressed woman in a fur coat and fur hat has just been reunited with her husband and she listens - with the rest of the world - to his story of beatings and degradation. At first she looks uncomprehending but this soon turns to dismay and then to tears.

121

The arrivals are shepherded inside the modern sports complex and are processed by the Croatian authorities. There is registration followed by medical examination. In the medical room, a man who is far from young is gently probed by a doctor. He flinches under examination. He has three broken ribs. "They broke one rib each day for three days. There was not one day they did not beat each of us – even the women."

In a gymnasium down the corridor second hand clothes and new underwear and socks are being distributed to a great scramble of humanity. Men with nothing - not even the clothes they no longer stand up in - hold up suits, trousers and shirts before arriving at sartorial decisions. The large netball court next door is laid out with iron beds in serried ranks, some 200 of them, to form a vast, improvised dormitory. Here the unclaimed will sleep.

Outside, the clamour from a rapidly growing crowd gets ever louder. Word of the officially unannounced arrival of the prisoners has spread through the Zagreb area via some sort of bush telegraph and hopefuls who have lost contact with friends or relatives from Vukovar are gathering in their hundreds. They press against the doors and windows hoping to recognise a face. At the main entrance an aid worker reads out the list of names. Just occasionally, there is an excited shout of identification. More usually a silence greets the names. And, when the list is read, there is a bitter chorus of wails from the disappointed. One woman collapses and is passed through the crowd.

All of a sudden, the mood of the crowd changes in a quite extraordinary and apparently united way. The mood of patient enquiry seems to change to one of shocked incredulity. It seems the people gathered cannot believe their loved ones are not secreted within. People start to shout and to push. Some shake their fists. The pressure on the doors increases and, with a protracted cracking noise, the hinges of the doors give way under the pressure. The police on the doors are swept away by the tide of humanity which tumbles and sweeps into the foyer of the complex. Eyes dart from side to side, bodies weave this way and that in search of friends or relatives. Most of the searchers are to be disappointed and ultimately they simply filter away into the night. Perhaps the next convoy . . .

I wondered what was to become of the unclaimed detritus of war. Those people whose homes - and maybe relatives - were gone for ever. The following day I went to the small town of Klancej, 56 km. from Zagreb on the border with Slovenia. Hemmed in by mountains, in the snow of winter it was a location of spectacular beauty. At first sight, the railway station was a typical small town terminus. The buildings were neatly kept and the stationmaster was impeccably turned out in his blue uniform with its red cap and his red flag. You might imagine the Orient Express pulling through in some Balkan time warp.

Across the tracks, some twenty or so carriages are standing. But there is something rather permanent about this aged, green-painted rolling stock: the steps down are supplemented by roughly hewn wooden steps and multi-coloured washing hangs out to dry from the windows.

For four months of this cruel winter, these carriages have been home to more than 100 refugees from the eastern Slavonia region around Vukovar. There is something different about these refugees. They are smartly dressed. You are made conscious of your own quite false preconceptions of the refugee. They are not necessarily pathetic creatures in loincloth or kaftan. These are recently affluent, middle class people who have lost their homes in a war which came swiftly and without warning sweeping aside dreams and security in its path.

Just 3 km. up the tracks from these improvised dwellings is the village of Kumrovec. In what now must be one of the great ironies of this divided and war torn country, there stands the perfectly preserved birthplace of Josep Broz Tito. The house is now closed up and the statue in the garden is boarded up and surrounded by sandbags. "We fear they will come and bomb it," explains the local schoolteacher. Who "they" are I am not quite sure. The architect of post-war Yugoslavia should be turning in his grave at the fate of the refugees of Klancej and all the hundreds of thousands like them.

10. ALL TANKED UP AT THE FRONT

There was a week when two remarkable women came into my life. One was young, graceful and beautiful. The other was old, small and toothless. It's a sort of story of Snow White and the dwarf. Superficially, these two very different women did have one thing in common - they had both taken up arms to fight for Croatia. But there any similarity - superficial or otherwise - ended.

In the town of Djakovo, on Croatia's battered eastern front, I found 24 year-old Snjezana Paradzikovic working at the military headquarters. Her name, literally translated, means Snow White but she was, in fact, dark and very beautiful. She came to Djakovo from the nearby village of Semeljci. "The Serbs from the next village were shooting at us all the time. I spent my time hiding in the cellar with my parents."

So, one day Snjezana decided the time had come and she went to the local military post and joined the National Guard. She was the only woman there. Two months later, she was transferred to the regional headquarters in Djakovo.

"I remain here to do my job until there is peace," she says quietly. Despite her initiative and her determination she is surprisingly shy and reserved - especially for a woman who works with hundreds of men around her all the time. This does not seem to bother her. "They make fun a little but most of them act quite properly."

Later in the day, she took me to her village. Despite the ceasefire which was supposed to be in operation throughout Croatia, the village had taken a barrage of 11 mortar shells during the night. Villagers were clearing up the debris. Snjezana's house had not been hit but shrapnel had sprayed over the roof.

124

We go to the frontline, just a kilometre or so up the road. One of the men hands Snjezana a Kalashnikov. Machine gun in hand, in her red beret and green camouflage uniform she cuts a stunning figure. There really is nothing quite like a pretty girl toting a machine gun. I suddenly feel all peculiar. The antidote came later.

I had heard in the bar of the Intercontinental in Zagreb rumours of a legendary grandmother down near the industrial town of Karlovac who commanded a tank with her sons and grandsons in the crew. Everybody seemed to have heard of her but nobody had actually ever met her. This surely seemed worth a look: it seemed to me like a *real* story. And so, bright and early the next morning, there I was zooming down a deserted motorway to Karlovac.

In fact, the game of *cherchez la femme* was not to be concluded anywhere near the town of Karlovac but enquiries at the local radio station revealed her to be 50 km. or so away, up at the front line. A pass from military headquarters, two AK-47 toting Guardsmen aboard, and we were in business in the Budget rentacar heading up into the snow covered hills.

Now I'm not crazy about speeding over snow covered and ice packed roads in the best of circumstances. The baleful advice of my companions didn't increase my confidence.

"Don't drive so slowly. It is very dangerous here. Crossfire."

Then the instruction. "Drive very slowly here. It is very dangerous." I looked around more than a trifle confused. There were some funny wire things sticking up through the snow all around us. "These mines. Not to make the wires move or boom-boom." Somewhere off to our left there was a burst of light machine gun fire and I held on to the wheel in grim concentration. I decided that the infractions of the local highways department at home would be a little more tolerable in future.

After an hour or so of this hair raising progress we came to Kamenica. Before the war there had been just a couple of dozen villagers. Now their number was supplemented by some 250 soldiers. As my car slithered to a halt in the main street - indeed the only street - the door of a humble single-storeyed peasant dwelling flew open to reveal Kamenica's devastating answer to General Rommel.

In her padded helmet and camouflage uniform there was the legendary Rozika Militic - indeed 60 years-old, wrinkled and toothless but, nevertheless, tank commanderess *extraordinaire*. Inside her home we quaffed *slivovich* and amid much laughing, joking and backslapping this remarkable woman told me of her life. Not content with raising six children - two boys and four girls - and running the family smallholding after the death of her husband, she grabbed the opportunity a couple of months ago to commandeer a captured Federal army T-55 tank.

It was brought to the village and her 32-year-old son, Matija, learned to drive the tank. None of them had any experience of anything more complex than a tractor but, undeterred by technology, the battered rustics sent to military headquarters in Karlovac for an instruction manual which was duly delivered. Long evenings were spent poring over the words and diagrams and soon the complexities were conquered.

Now the tank boasted a full crew of local villagers and it was parked just below the brow of a hill overlooking their homes. "If the Serbs wish to come here they had better look out!" declared the indomitable Rozika with a a sweep of her hand and a wide toothless grin. We downed glass after glass of the home made spirit with the toast "Zivi u miru" - *Live in Peace*. This was clearly going to go on for some time and so, with a flash of inspiration, I produced my emergency hip flask of scotch whisky. My courteous hosts enthusiastically downed same but I could tell it was not quite to their taste and, the cycle of drinks broken, we climbed the hill to the tank.

It nestled snuggly below the brow of a hill enjoying a commanding view of the valley below. In honour of the latest ceasefire - which was noisily punctuated every ten minutes or so by bursts of machine gun fire which were cheerfully ignored by Rozika - the T-55 was shrouded in its canvas covers. These were eagerly drawn back by its proud owners, like some family car drawn out of the garage for the neighbours to see.

I asked if the cover might be removed from the mouth of the gun but this, apparently, was against the ceasefire regulations. In the distance there was the crump of something which, to me, sounded suspiciously like a mortar explosion. Rozika grinned and waved her AK-47 assault rifle as she adopted a series of remarkably professional poses for the camera. All the while her crew swarm enthusiastically over their charge priming, tweaking and whatever else you do to set a tank in motion.

Rozika hoisted her aged bones up onto the front of the tank and lowered herself down the hatch. The last image of her was of a bony hand extended up through the hatch, a defiant V for Victory sign described through the air. Truly stirring stuff. Now for the big moment - moving the metal mammoth up to combat position at the brow of the hill.

A sort of feeble whinnying sound emits from somewhere underneath the armour plate. Then there is silence. More sounds of evident distress and it becomes abundantly clear we have a stranded leviathan on our hands. The battery is flat, I am phlegmatically advised by the commander from the depths of her charge. So, alas, no demonstration today. The war is definitely on hold.

Now you know that uneasy feeling when you have just a tiny, nagging suspicion that your leg is being pulled . . . It took a few more home-made plum brandies before I could finally banish the uneasy thought from my mind.

Rozika hardly qualified as a secret weapon, although she was undoubtedly a formidable propaganda tool. Three men I met in Djakovo in the Spring of '92 were in an altogether different league. They had very much been Croatia's secret weapon. Their exploits had become almost legendary in the embattled republic. Even the mention of 'The Black Crows from Livane' was said to awaken dread and terror in some Serbian quarters.

127

Yet their weaponry could hardly have been said to be devastating and it was most certainly not out of the last decade of the 20th century. Their aerial adventures were, in fact, more out of *The Boys' Own Paper* or *Biggles Flies Again*, and their weapons and tactics were straight from the First World War.

The Black Crows were a group of former parachutists in the Yugoslav Federal Air Force who formed themselves into the very first unit in the Croatian Air Force - known as the HRZ. The seven members of the unit were all members of the local flying club in battered Osijek and they commandeered a handful of small Russian-built Antonov crop spraying 'planes. After Osijek's aerodrome was bombed, they marked out secret landing places in secluded fields and forests along the eastern front and were careful not to use any one landing place for more than two or three days at a time.

They had no conventional bombs or armaments. Instead, they took up 100 litre gas canisters packed in dynamite and simply threw them out of the 'planes onto enemy positions. On impact they exploded with devastating force turning the heavy metal gas canisters into terrifying shrapnel bombs.

During the long and bitter siege of Vukovar they flew over the city dropping urgently needed medical supplies by parachute. On other missions they dropped one-use only anti-tank guns, known as *armbrusts*, by parachute to the beleagured defenders. Their leader Babac - this was only a code name as they never revealed their real names - was 21 years in the Federal Air Force but even he was stunned by the ferocity of the attack on Vukovar. "Flying over the city it seemed like the ground was boiling with all the explosions."

Much of their time after the implementation of the January 'ceasefire' was taken up with transferring up to six wounded soldiers at a time from the field dressing stations on the eastern front to hospitals in the capital of Zagreb.

Their activities were cloaked in secrecy just as their 'planes and gliders were covered in camouflage netting in the forest

128

clearings. You understood why when they told you that they were seven in number only six months previously: now only three of them survive. Two pilots and two parachutists have died. Their blue arm badges bear the insignia of a black crow with a red beak descending by parachute above a gold cross made up of seven diamond shapes - three across and four up the way indicating the living and the dead.

It's a miracle they survive at all against the Mig jets of the Federal Air Force. The Mig radar, however, is not built to track such primitive planes - it can only track objects travelling at a minimum of 175 m.p.h so the Black Crows cruise the skies in their lumbering aircraft at just 100 m.p.h.! The sophisticated Migs cannot attack unless they have a visual sighting.

The Black Crows were soon to become redundant but their exploits will live on. In the short term, they had certainly had one effect throughout the frontline areas of eastern Croatia. By the Spring of '92 you simply couldn't find a portable gas canister anywhere . . .

11. DON'T THEY KNOW IT'S CHRISTMAS?

It is the season of goodwill to all men and a small Christmas tree illuminates the bleak corridor outside the mortuary at Djakovo Hospital, just a few kilometres from Croatia's eastern front. The bodies of the three Croatian National Guardsmen were brought in around midday on stretchers and laid out in the white-tiled room for postmortem. Still dressed in their dark green camouflage uniforms, their features were frozen at the moment of death. The yellowed pallor and the staring expressions - of seeming disbelief at their fate - lent them the appearance of skilfully executed waxworks. But waxworks they were not. And brutal execution was what had cut short their lives but a few hours previously.

Their features aged in death, these three young men were just 23, 25 and 28 years old. They had all lived in the same village of Sodolovci; they had all been friends and they had all joined up together three months ago to protect their village from the Serbian irregulars, the Chetniks who had started to infiltrate the area. With the fall of Vukovar last month, the front line gradually edged nearer and nearer to their village and now the front line fighting is all around: reaching the beleagured towns of nearby Vinkovci and Osijek.

The previous night the three had set off from their village on a night patrol. When they had not returned by dawn, search parties were sent out. Villagers combing the woods discovered their bodies in a shallow grave. It was evident they had been shot but the full horror of their death was only to become apparent with the postmortem.

Their commanding officer arrived. Solidly built, self assured you could sense he was a leader of men. No time was wasted, he had done this before. Deftly, he emptied the pockets; useful items of

equipment were retrieved for future use; documents and papers
laid aside. Then the bodies were stripped. This was heavy work.
Rigor mortis had set in and the bodies had to be cumbersomely
manhandled by the officer and two young female doctors.

Soon the manner of their death became apparent. All had been
shot: many times in both arms but these wounds were not the
cause of death. Their bodies had been cut with knives and then
two had been finished off with knife wounds to the heart. The
third had died when his head was battered and crushed,
possibly with a rifle butt.

Dr Shelko Milic, head of surgery at Djakovo Hospital, was in no
doubt about the sequence of the night's events. "These men
were taken prisoner. Some of the wounds may have come in the
fight but they were shot in the arms later, tortured and then
killed."

The door to the mortuary was opened to let in the cold fresh air
and to dispel the rising stench. Every so often, the young girls
would go out into the fresh air in their bloodied white overalls,
wipe their brows, gulp down the the clean air, and then return
to their bloody work.

The soldiers and doctors standing around the door are
transfixed by the horror. Nobody notices a little old man making
his way to the open door. He looks old - very old. Old enough to
have seen three of these wars. His face is deeply wrinkled and
weatherbeaten - the face of a man who worked his life on the
land. His jacket - probably his best - is a couple of sizes too big
and flaps around. Too late the soldiers see him but he is too
quick for them. Lowering his head, he weaves between them
like a hare in flight and then is at the mortuary door peering in
at a vision of hell. There is silence for a brief moment as he
takes in the scene and then a desperate, piercing wail. "Mou
sin, Mou sin . " *My son, my son*.

Led from the mortuary, he breaks free from the soldiers and,
clutching his head in his hands, he runs to and fro, hither and
thither, wailing piteously. Tears are now running in rivulets

131

down those aged wrinkles on his face. He is inconsolable. All attempts at comfort are shrugged away.

Other relatives arrive. One young wife collapses at the door of the mortuary and is carried away by two soldiers. The doctors carry on with their gruesome work. And, all the while, the old man continues his anguished dash around the mortuary building.

Half an hour or so later, I prepare to leave. The doctors are wiping the blood from the walls of the mortuary. Dr Milic sucks pensively on a gold cigarette holder. "Yes, I am a professional and I have seen this before. But it is still very difficult for me." There are tears in the eyes of a soldier standing at the door. The commanding officer makes unrepeatable observations about the Chetniks. And the old man continues his anguished progress, repeating over and over again, in frenzied disbelief those same two words. "Mou sin! Mou sin!"

In themselves, casualty figures convey little. They are but cold statistics despite their scale. Before Christmas, the unofficial estimated death toll in Croatia was estimated at between six and ten thousand dead. Even then, I reckoned it might probably be nearer 50,000 when all the shallow graves had been emptied and all the rubble of the hundreds of devastated villages had been sifted. By way of example, it was common knowledge in Zagreb the week before Christmas that there had just been a terrible and tragic reverse. Near to the village of Pokupsko, just 28 km. from Zagreb, an attempted Croatian offensive had gone horribly wrong. Hundreds of young soldiers of but a few weeks training - in reality engineers, teachers, lawyers and clerks - had been forced back to the banks of the fast flowing River Kupa. There, in the terror of flight, they drowned in the river. The disaster was not admitted to by the Ministry of Information: they said two men died. A soldier who was there said 490. And at lunch in Zagreb those around the table knew half a dozen who had died there.

Remote from such horrors, it is difficult enough to appreciate the deep wounds left on all the living who will mourn 490 men,

61 Shattered house, Turanj. The sad abandoned image of a young girl whose bedroom this once was.

62 On their return to Vinkovci, this couple find their home is beyond repair.

63 Impossible job? Clearing up at Nustar.

64 Humour in war. Police checkpoint, Bosanski Brod.

65 A UN jeep passes a destroyed house at Toran, near Pakrac in Sector West.

66 EC monitors at Turanj, Christmas Day. Eric Gautier (left).

67 Captain Ned Middleton of the Royal Army Pay Corps, attached to UNPROFOR, on his white-painted UN tricycle at sub-HQ Pleso.

68 Bagpipers of the Canadian contingent, November company, UNPROFOR Sector West, Sirac.

69 Outside the mortuary at Djakovo, Christmas week. The body of this woman's husband lies inside.

70 The grisly scene inside the mortuary.

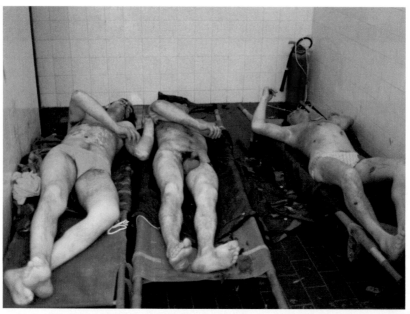

let alone the 10,000, the 50,000, or whatever, who have died in just six months of bitter and bloody conflict. The scale of the tragedy is vast as to be quite incomprehensible. The deaths, the injuries, the brutality and the damage is is so enormous as to render it difficult to adequately describe.

There is, however, one simple uncluttered image which does convey it all in microcosm. An image which conveys more than all the bald casualty figures. That image of an old, old man, his head in his hands, running around the mortuary building at Djakavo locked in his own frenzy of personal despair. It must have been a bitter Christmas in Sodolovci.

In the silences between the singing and the prayers you could hear outside the impatient chatter of machine gun fire, the explosion of mortars and the dull crump of heavy artillery. The singing was loud and passionate, as if in direct defiance of the incessant reminder of the horrors being enacted outside the Franciscan Church of the Holy Trinity in the town of Karlovac. This was the reality of a mist-laden, drizzly Christmas Day in Croatia.

The assembled worshippers must, superficially at least, have resembled any congregation elsewhere in Europe that Christmas morning. Sprucely turned out children, their cheeks made red in the sub-zero temperatures outside; peasant women and widows in black; townswomen in their furs and hats; old men in their best suits. But, as you looked around that packed church a few minutes before morning mass was due to begin, there were no young men, few fathers and certainly no men of military age. Then, just as the service was about to begin, men in uniform filtered in through the congregation. They came in twos and threes until the church was packed. There they stood crowded into the nave in their green camouflage uniforms, heads bowed and hands crossed respectfully. Here and there were the German-made dark brown uniforms of the 110th Brigade which included the foreigners who have come to fight here and Serbs who have elected to stay and fight with the Croatians. And, in stark contrast, conspicuous in its pristine white, was the uniform of a solitary EC monitor.

At the end of the nave, where you would normally have been able to see the ornamental stained glass in all its glory, sandbags were piled to the roof. The frontline is only a couple of kilometres from this 17th century church with its painted frescoes, finely wrought pews and its prized black Madonna. The 80,000 inhabitants of Karlovac have been under daily bombardment since September 15. Whether or not by Divine intervention, this beautiful church has thus far been spared but all those gathered there must have been aware of its fragility, its awful vulnerability in the face of devastating modern weapons of war.

Even for an outsider, essentially uninvolved in the day to day traumas of this war torn community, the service was a deeply moving experience. Prayers for Croatia, prayers for their own community, prayers for the soldiers, prayers for the bereaved and prayers for the dead. Even a prayer for the journalists killed in the war. And for the EC monitors.

Some of the women cried. But, as I looked around, it was clear that most of the soft, gentle sobbing was coming from the soldiers. From the men in uniform, none of whom could have been soldiers for any more than six months, and who had seen so much in such a short time. I had only once before seen the faces of men like that before - two days previously at that mortuary in Djkakovo. And I knew why these men were crying.

Christmas lunch had not been on the menu when we set out that morning but it rather unexpectedly appeared when we pitched up at military headqurters in Karlovac to collect our escort to the frontline. In the mess, soup, chicken and vegetables, salad and cake, were all washed down with an excellent Dalmatian wine.

A couple of kilometres up the road in the village of Turanj, just across the river from Karlovac, they were also lunching - and fighting - when we arrived in the afternoon. A couple of tank crews, clearly expecting not to do any business that day, were singing noisily in the kitchen of a farmhouse, an empty bottle of Kentucky whisky on the table. In a stone barn across the road a hot Christmas meal was being delivered to the couple of dozen or so soldiers billeted there.

I had last been in Turanj in the middle of September and had sat outside on the terrace of a neat cafe in the warm autumn sunshine. That same cafe - like all the buildings around - was now totally devastated: its roof blown in, its interior gutted by fire, the outside pockmarked by bullets and the striped awnings hanging down in shreds. This village was now the killing ground with just two or three hundred metres dividing the protagonists. Nobody now lived in this once prosperous village which had once been full of people who went to work in the textile factories and engineering works of Karlovac. Within sight of Turanj is the Jugoturbina works. In June it employed 10,000 people. That day, after three months of wilful damage, there were just 200 workers.

There is a heavy, damp mist. This we are glad of. It cuts down the sniper activity and observers can't call in the mortars. The mud lies thick and glutinous and we pick our way gingerly through mud, shrapnel, shell casings and the general detritus of war. A shell lands noisily a couple of hundred yards or so up the road, setting light to a once neat, whitewashed house. We take cover in the barn where Christmas dinner is being devoured. The soldiers sleep here in shifts before moving up the road to do battle. In the corner is a Christmas tree complete with decoration and lights - the only light in the room - next to a radio operator intercepting morse messages in the gloom.

One of their number has been killed a few hours previously in the yard outside by a mortar bomb and they have just finished burying him. Nevertheless, morale seems remarkably good. Or, at least, there is much bravado about. A young soldier approaches and touches my arm.

As I look into his eyes I know that I am looking into the face of a deeply troubled man. Jadranko is 21. He speaks perfect

135

English and he desperately wants to talk. Conscripted into the army just a few weeks previously, he had finished three years of a five year course in shipbuilding engineering. "I know I must fight for Croatia. But really I want to learn. To live." I recognise that he is looking for some reassurance from me; that he instinctively feels I will understand his unhappiness and fear. But our talk is interrupted by the guffaws of his fellows who are, I realise, poking fun at him. The commanding officer waves me awy from him, lest I become contaminated. Jadranko slinks away into the darkness of a corner, retreating into his own misery: the weakest animal in the pack.

Christmas Day brings Turanj its own footnote in the history books. The very last convoy of Federal troops to retreat from Croatian territory under the supervision of EC monitors leaves here mid-afternoon to cross over into Bosnia, just three kilometres down the road. This rearguard is made up of the mine disposal team and their equipment from Pleso barracks, near Zagreb. They remained behind to try and clear the mines from around the barracks. The problem was they laid the mines without charting them and so three of their number had died trying to locate them in the frosty ground of winter.

Passing the convoy through the lines turns out to be a tricky operation. Although only a few hundred metres separate the two sides, communication is currently only being conducted through the barrel of a gun. My respect for the EC efforts improves dramatically when the white jeep with its blue insignia simply drives up the road into the mist, its klaxon hooting noisily. It comes under fire and after a couple of minutes turns back. One of the monitors points out to the Croatians that they have failed to remove all the mines - there are still deadly Saracen anti-personnel mines on the road. The Croatians give the distinct impression they aren't that bothered.

The French leader of the EC team - Eric Gautier - rounds on them and addresses them like so many naughty children. "Right, I tell you what I am going to do. I am going back up that road and I will stand beside those mines and wave the convoy around."

And that is precisely what he did. He had guts that Frenchman. That was the only truly Christian act I witnessed in Karlovac that Christmas Day. But why did he do it? Not for Croatia, not for the retreating Serbs. Certainly not for Europe. I think I know why. He was that EC man bowed in prayer in the Church of the Holy Trinity on Christmas morning.

12. BLUE BERETS

When Colonel Christopher Price returned to his white-painted British army Landrover, parked in the streets of Zagreb, there was a handwritten notice on the windscreen of the UN vehicle. "GET IN OR GET OUT Signed The Croatian People", it read. The admonitory notice - physical evidence of the ambivalence marking the UN operation in what used to be Yugoslavia - was now stuck to the wall of his makeshift office at Zagreb's Pleso Airport, underneath his 'battle' map of the former republic. It was there as a constant reminder of the tinderbox nature of local sensibilities.

Forty-four year old Scot Colonel Price was the Commander-in-Chief of the British contingent of the UNPROFOR. Born at Twynholm, Kirkcudbrightshire, he was educated at Glenalmond and commissioned in 1967. In 1988 he became the commander of the 1st Battalion Gordon Highlanders before transfer in 1991 to the Joint Chiefs of the Defence Staff at Greenwich. He is a career soldier in the modern vein. It shows in his frankness when you fire off a difficult question.

"Yes, this is a heck of a job here. It's very difficult to keep a peace with two opposing sides who distrust each other so much. As for disarming them . . .". He and his colleagues are aware that irregulars on both sides have now poured themselves into police uniforms in the four UN Sectors. The delayed - some might say stalled - nature of the UN operation did not help either.

"When I arrived on March 8 there was lots of flag waving. We got a big welcome. But three months later we are still not fully operational and people are quite naturally beginning to ask when we are going to get started."

Not that this was due to any lack of will on the part of the UN. It was purely a matter of logistics; a reflection of an assortment of operational problems. The choice of Sarajevo as UN HQ was disastrous. By the end of April, UN personnel in the besieged city were virtually cut off and under constant bombardment in the worst attack to be launched on a European capital since the Second War. Specifically for the deployment of the British contingent (BRITCON), the British general election, by multi-party agreement, delayed the despatch of most of the British force of 800; principally medical units and logistics people. "Both major political parties agreed not to commit the other irrevocably to this most difficult of operations," admitted Graeme Hammond a senior Ministry of Defence spokesman permanently attached to BRITCON. His very presence on the ground underlined the dangers and sensitivities involved in the operation.

The thirty members of BRITCON then in place at Pleso were joined on June 8 by the rest of the force, for whose arrival they had been preparing over the previous three months. Every day, Colonel Price and his men - engineers, ordnance men and experts with specific skills - had been out into the UN protected areas, formerly the battlegrounds of Croatia. The fighting was now not continuous: rather it was sporadic and unpredictable. And all the more dangerous for that.

Not only do the protagonists in the conflict distrust each other but that hostility often extends to the UN troops. Now 'civvies' were worn for a night out in Zagreb. In Sector West, outside the totally destroyed town of Pakrac, a middle-aged woman waxed eloquent on the relations enjoyed between the Serbian irregulars and the UN from behind the counter of her village shop. "They say the UN supply the Chetniks with beer and cigarettes." And in Sector East, where a Russian general is in control, a Croatian soldier made an even more bitter observation. "They are playing football with the Chetniks." You have to understand they take their football very seriously in Croatia.

The men in this, the largest, UN force ever to be deployed in Europe are drawn from 31 countries. As unlikely a mixture as you might hope to meet: from the UK to Argentina, from Canada

139

to Czechoslovakia, from Jordan to Nepal. Theirs is a difficult series of roles as interposers, intermediaries, observers and peacekeepers in an area which, indubitably, demanded peacemakers rather than that more passive genre. In the former war zones they are, deliberately, thick on the ground: the distinctive white vehicles constantly on patrol for both sides to see. Any infringements of the ceasefire are immediately reported to Sector HQ by radio and thence by satellite to New York. In this way information of the infractions of some trigger happy irregular or Guardsman can be in the Secretary General's office within minutes and extension of any conflict halted, if necessary, through the highest political or military channels.

Sometimes the UN men themselves come under fire. This is endlessly frustrating for highly trained military men forbidden to fight back lest they become a third party to the dogfight. The Canadian contingent found this out within a bare two hours of their arrival. A company of the 3rd Infantry Battalion of the Royal Canadian Regiment was shelled by one side or the other as it set up camp at Sirac in Sector West. The Croats blamed the Serbian irregulars, and vice versa. What was clear to the UN men was that they had been deliberately shelled for propaganda purposes: so that their attackers might have something dramatic for which to blame the other side. 'November' company was now expertly dug-in in a network of underground bunkers protected by well-filled sandbag emplacements.

The logistics of organising a multi-national force of this type are formidable. When deployment was completed later in June, there were 14,000 troops on the ground. The initial error of judgement in establishment of the operation's headquarters was been followed by relatively more minor problems: the Kenyan troops arrived with nought but their shorts and shirts and were sent home; the Nepalese arrived without vehicles or equipment - but were fitted out with former East German transport. In the face of practical difficulties in a land of which they have no knowledge, you find men to be enormously resourceful. The Paymaster attached to the British contingent, Captain Ned Middleton, finding himself without any transport negotiated locally for a war damaged ice cream vendor's tricycle on a six month loan and repair basis. Overnight it was repaired and painted UN white, to transport him to bank and back at the cost of no more than a modicum of physical effort. When I flew into Sarajevo Airport two months later I saw that it was in use on the tarmac there.

Croatia is grown tired of war. Of that there can be no doubt. Tired of devastation, waste and human tragedy on a scale unwitnessed by Europe since 1945. All the UN men you meet admit to being appalled by the devastation they have seen. At one moment, they are captivated by the beauty of the landscape, the next they are confronted by the realities of a mediaeval war fought with 20th century weaponry: the shell shattered buildings, the refugees, the bitterness and the hatred. The presence of the UN men has brought an uneasy truce for the moment and life has in subtle ways returned to something approaching normalcy. The shelling of Osijek on the eastern front ceased after nine months and the fountains were switched on in the shattered main square. Around Sector West, the police now stop you to courteously hand you a speeding ticket rather than wave machine guns at you at armed checkpoints.

In the spa town of Daruvar, the old and the infirm queue to fill containers with warm, sulphurous water in front of the UN headquarters for Sector West. In the nearby Thermal Hotel, the blue berets of the UN weave their careful way around the limbless boys; the Croatian soldiers struggling with their newly-issued crutches. Outside, a man on a bicycle with only one arm threads his way with amazing new found dexterity through the maze of white-painted jeeps and APCs of the UN's 1200 strong Canadian contingent. These injured boys' short-lived careers as soldiers in an army founded exactly one year ago are at an end.

The Canadians, Swedes, Danes and French at Daruvar are too diplomatic to make more than veiled observations about the warring parties but their distaste for the lack of military discipline, security and professionalism is evident. Even a non-military observer can see the differences between the Ramboesque local forces and the UN professionals: it shows in the uniforms, the salutes, the tightly packed sandbags, the

141

textbook defences, and the high level of alert. At UNPROFOR HQ in Daruvar I asked the sentry how he was getting on today. "I'm not at liberty to disclose that information, Sir," came the tight lipped response. His Croatian counterpart would have offered you a slug of slivovitch. The Canadians, like the Swedes and the Danes, have been involved in virtually every UN peacekeeping operation. You sense that the peacekeeping role comes naturally to them rather unlike the British who have, throughout recent history, been accustomed to taking sides, fighting and assuming a more direct role in conflict whether in Northern Ireland, Cyprus or the Falklands.

When you ask Captain Douglas Martin, Canadian "officer for public affairs" about that country's commitment he points out that it is total, "We have participated in every single UN peacekeeping operation." And his own personal commitment? He seems to have no doubts there either. "Blessed are the peacemakers:for they shall be called the children of God. Matthew 5:9."

APPENDIX I

CHRONOLOGY

1980

Death of Marshall Tito, founder of post-war Yugoslavia

1981

Riots in Kosovo

1983

Alija Izetbegovic and other Muslim leaders in Bosnia jailed

1987

Slobodan Milosevic becomes President of Serbia

1988

General strike in Kosovo

Janez Jansa jailed by military court in Ljubljana. Pressure for secession grows in Slovenia and Croatia

1989

JNA goes into Kosovo

Slovene assembly amends consitution to allow for secession

1990

April Elections in Croatia and Slovenia

In Croatia HDZ gains 67.5% of seats and DEMOS coalition wins in Slovenia

September Serbia abolishes Kosovo and Vojvodina autonomy

December 23 Plebiscite in Slovenia reveals 99% vote for independence

1991

May 2 Widespread violence breaks out in Croatia.

May 6 JNA soldier dies outside naval base at Split as 30,000 demonstrators attack perimeter.

May 7 Fighting in eastern Croatia and Dalmatia. 18 have now died since May 2.

June 25 Slovenia and Croatia declare independence.

June 26 New signs erected and flags hoisted at Slovenian border crossings. Federal tanks reported on the move. Brnik airport closed by Federal authorities at 1200. Evening independence celebrations in Ljubljana.

June 27 More JNA tanks leave their barracks in Slovenia and Croatia. JNA attempts to wrest control of border posts. JNA helicopter shot down over Ljubljana after circling parliament building.

June 28 Attack on Ljubljana airport (Brnik), roadblocks at Sentilj and Medvedjek on highway to Zagreb. Evening clashes around Brnik.

June 29 Attack on Slovenian police at border crossing at Skofije. Clashes around military airbase at Cerklje. Federal army ultimatum for surrender by 0900 next day. Secret night session of Slovenian Parliament.

June 30 Air raid warnings sound in Ljubljana at 0900.

July 1 Ceasefire in operation. Many JNA soldiers surrendering. Barracks and ammunition dump at Crni Vrh blown up by JNA.

July 2 Radio and TV transmitters bombed. Tank formations leave Jastrabarsko, Varazdin and Zagreb (Croatia) and launch attack on Slovenia. Croatian civilians petrol bomb tanks leaving Marshall Tito Barracks, Zagreb. Tanks on the move from Belgrade.

July 3 Tank movements from Serbia stop after Western pressure. Margaret Thatcher contacts President George Bush who exerts pressure for end to conflict.

July 4 JNA forces withdrawing to barracks.

July 7 EEC-brokered Brioni Agreement brings end to conflict in Slovenia. Tension rising in Croatia; fighting in Tenje, near Osijek.

144

July 11 Fighting in the streets of Osijek.

July 19 Serbian irregular forces attack Vinkovci and Vukovar

July 26 Heavy fighting breaks out around Glina between Croatian Guardsmen and Serbian irregulars. Six Croatian policemen die at Struga. Battles for bridges over Danube connecting Croatia and Serbia.

August 1 Eighty Croatian policemen killed in fierce battle at Dalj on the Danube in eastern Croatia.

August 18 Heavy fighting starts in Pakrac, western Slavonija.

August 24 Attacks on Vukovar intensified: city bombed.

September 15 Army barracks throughout Croatia put under siege. Air raid sirens sound in Zagreb as Migs overfly the capital.

September 20 JNA launches major assault - with reported 700 tanks supported by infantry - on eastern front around Osijek, Vukovar and Vinkovci.

September 21 JNA forces enter Petrinja.

September 28 Bjelovar barracks captured by Croatians after heavy fighting.

September 30 New JNA military offensive involving armoured columns launched on eastern front.

October 1 JNA commences attack on Dubrovnik.

October 7 Federal air force bombs Presidential palace, Zagreb.

October 19 *Medecins sans Frontières* aid convoy reaches besieged Vukovar.

October 16 Major attack on Luzac heralds push on Vukovar.

November 4 Fiercest attack yet on Sisak. Refinery and industrial zone ablaze. Heavy fighting around Nova Gradiska.

November 17 Vukovar near surrender.

November 19 Vukovar finally falls. Osijek and Vinkovci now Serbian objectives.

November 20 False report from Reuters of alleged massacre of 41 schoolchildren by Croatian soldiers.

November 22 Dobroslav Paraga, leader of the opposition Croatian HSP, arrested in Zagreb. Tension high in the capital.

November 26 New area of attack opened by Serbian forces on Podravska Slatina in bid to cut supply route to eastern front.

November 29 JNA quits barracks in Zagreb.

December 11 Croatian forces announce significant gains in western Slavonia around Lipik and Nova Gradiska. Enemy now being held on other fronts.

December 18 News breaks of horrific massacre by Chetniks at Vocin, western Slavonia.

December 20 Yugoslav Prime Minister Ante Markovic resigns over allocation of 81% of budget to armed forces.

December 21 Serbs in BiH declare their own republic.

December 25 Last JNA troops leave Croatian held territory under EC sponsored withdrawal over frontline positions at Turanj.

December 27 Heavy attacks on Karlovac, south of Zagreb.

1992

January 3 Fifteenth ceasefire takes effect in Croatia.

January 7 Federal air force Mig 21 shoots down EC helicopter north of Zagreb killing all five observers aboard.

January 13 Vatican recognises Croatia and Slovenia.

January 14 UN military observers arrive in Croatia.

January 15 EC recognition of Slovenia and Croatia takes effect

January 22 Macedonian parliament votes to withdraw representatives from Yugoslav state parliament in Belgrade.

146

January 24 Bosnian parliament votes to proceed with referendum on independence.

February 18 UN Secretary-General formally recommends UN peacekeeping force of 14,000 for Yugoslavia.

February 24 Muslim and Croat leaders in BiH call on JNA to withdraw.

February 25 Explosion at Croation offices in Bosnian town of Odzaci.

February 29 Two day referendum on independence for BiH starts. Serbs erect barricades outside Bosanski Brod.

March 1 Shooting at a Serbian wedding in Sarajevo. First barricades go up in Sarajevo.

March 2 Bosanski Brod shelled. Serbs fire on peace demonstrators in Sarajevo.

March 5 Rallies for peace in Sarajevo.

March 10 UNPROFOR General Nambiar arrives in Zagreb.

March 16 Advance teams of UN peacekeepers setting up bases in Croatia.

March 26 Heavy fighting erupts in Bosanski Brod.

March 27 Serbs in Bosnia proclaim their own constitution.

April 3 Fighting in northern Bosnia. Serb irregulars attack Bijeljina. Barricades erected around Banja Luka.

April 6 New fighting in Sarajevo after snipers attack peace demonstrators. EC ministers decide to recognise BiH as an independent state.

April 8 Federal air force launches attacks throughout Bosnia.

April 21 Widespread fighting in Sarajevo: shelling and street fighting.

April 27 Serbia and Montenegro proclaim creation of new Yugoslav state.

April 30 Bridges connecting Bosnia and Croatia at Brcko and Bosanski Samac destroyed.

May 2 EC peace monitor killed near Mostar.

147

May 11 EC announces withdrawal of ambassadors from Belgrade in protest against continued siege of Sarajevo.

May 12 EC monitors pull out of Sarajevo. Red Cross prepares to pull out.

May 17 of UN peacekeepers pulls out of Sarajevo.

May 27 Sarajevo bread queue mortared by Serbs with heavy loss of life. Harrowing TV pictures bring pressure for sanctions against Serbia.

May 29 Serbian forces re-commence bombardment of Dubrovnik.

May 30 UN votes for sanctions against Serbia and Montenegro.

June 5 JNA evacuate barracks in Sarajevo.

June 8 Main body of British contingent of UNPROFOR arrives in Croatia. UN Security Council votes to reopen Sarajevo Airport for humanitarian relief.

June 16 BiH and Croatia announce military alliance. Croatian fighters regain control of Mostar.

June 20 BiH formally declares state of war as first step to general mobilisation.

June 27 Crown Prince Alexander Karadjordjevic returns to Belgrade.

June 28 100,000 take part in DEPOS demonstration against Milosevic regime in Belgrade. French President Francois Mitterand lands at Sarajevo Airport: anniversary of assassination of Crown Prince Ferdinand at Sarajevo.

June 29 Canadian UN troops leave Daruvar, Croatia, for overland reinforcement of Sarajevo Airport now opening to mercy traffic. First, French, relief plane lands Sarajevo.

July 10 NATO, WEU and CSCE leaders meeting in Helsinki decide on naval blockade of Serbia and Montenegro.

July 17 British Foreign Secretary Douglas Hurd briefly visits Sarajevo. Two French UN peacekeepers die near Zadar, Croatia, when their jeep hits a mine. Four thousand Bosnian refugees trapped in train outside Zagreb as all overwhelmed countries in the region deny refuge. UNHCR confirms three million people forced from their homes by the first year of fighting in what was Yugoslavia.

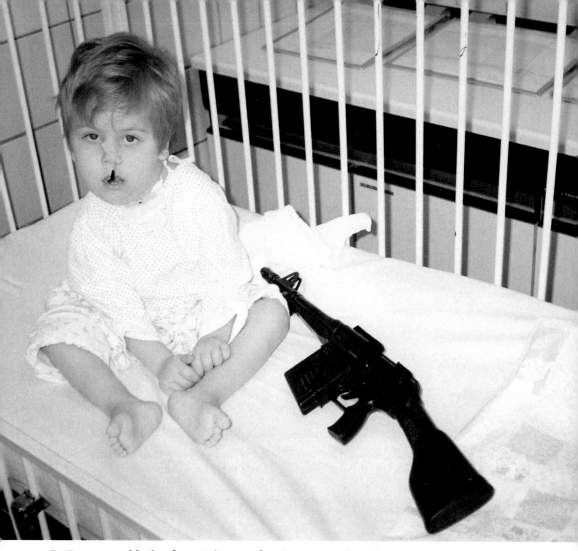

71 Four year-old Alen from Valpovo refused to give up his life-size toy machine gun at the childrens' hospital in Zagreb.

72 This tragic nine year-old from Vinkovci had shrapnel fragments lodged in his brain.

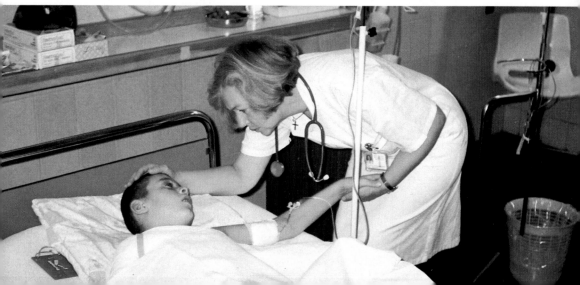

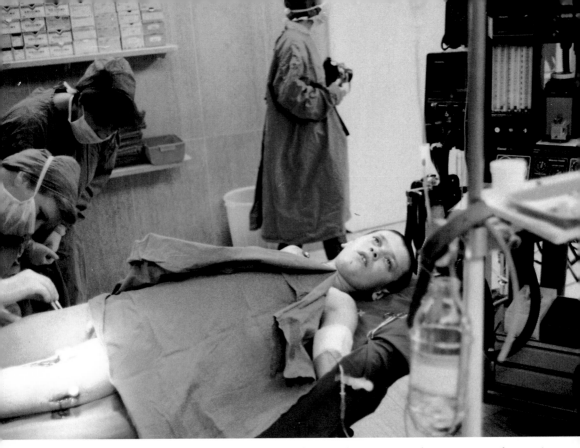

73-4 Thirteen year-old Aleksander from Pakrac in the operating theatre at Zagreb's Institute for Mothers and Children. He was injured by shrapnel. The windows are taped over against air attack.

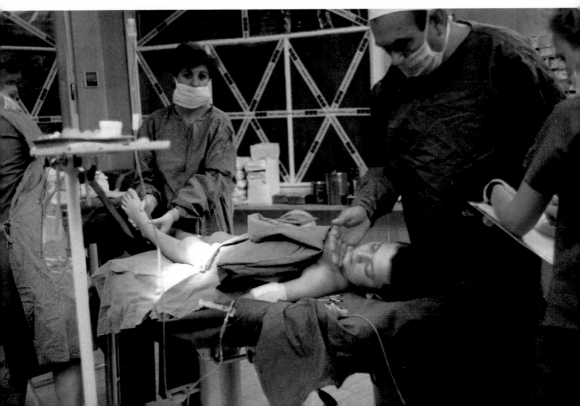

75 This boy flees from Bosnia at Gunja.

76 A Muslim girl flees from Bosnia across the bridge at Gunja.

77 House burning near Odzak,
northern Bosnia, May.

78 A Serbian house destroyed by
Croats in the countryside near to
Bosanski Brod.

79 Burning house, Bosanski Brod.

APPENDIX II

A NOTE ON THE STRATEGY
OF THE WAR

If one accepts that the wars in Slovenia, Croatia and Bosnia Herzegovina were premeditated and precipitated by political and military planners in Belgrade, then a basic outline of strategy would run as follows.

Following the declarations of independence by Slovenia and Croatia on June 25 1991, it was adjudged necessary in Belgrade to activate plans already made around 1987-88 to deal with such eventualities. The JNA had at its disposal some 180,000 men comprising 78,600 regular officers and 101,400 soldiers: conscripts aged between 17 and 22. Of the 1,880 tanks in the JNA, some 250 were stationed in Slovenia at the outbreak of hostilities and they were supplemented by a further 100 from Croatia. Slovenia's strategic importance in terms of its total control of Yugoslav borders with Italy and Austria required action to sieze border posts. This was largely achieved within a short period of 24 hours by the use of helicopter-borne assault troops. The operations of tanks deployed from barracks in Vrhnika and Ljubljana were severely curtailed by the rapid erection of barricades by well-briefed civilians and police. Slovene Territorial Defence Forces were well equipped and mobilised swiftly and effectively: 15,000 men were engaged in the first day of the conflict and by the end of the war 35,100 had been involved. A total of 7,100 Slovenian police were also used. They had a total of 3 TAM armoured cars and four helicopters. Other armament included 7.65mm. pistols and light machine guns: mainly Kalashnikovs, MP, M 14.5 and a few Heckler & Kochs. The Territorial Forces' most effective single weapon was the German one-use only *armbrust* which achieved an almost 100% success rate in the hands of inexperienced operators. Its magnetically guided missile, fired within the weapon's operational range of around 100 metres, proved a thorough tank killer and within 48 hours all the JNA tanks were either dug in, destroyed or confined to barracks.

Air power proved similarly ineffective. The attack on Brnik airport was psychologically effective but, in practical terms, a pathetic operation,

149

the most significant effect being the destruction of a row of expensive cars in the car park. Attacks on broadcasting and transmitting facilities were similarly ineffective and TV Slovenija was never obliged to leave the air. Conscript troops were - probably wisely - never committed to the fight. Western political pressure ultimately brought the conflict to an end after only ten days. The blitzkrieg attack on Slovenia had failed and there was no prospect of carrying through a longer term war against a united and ethnically homogenous population.

The situation in Croatia was somewhat different. In June and July members of the disaffected Serbian minority rose up in what was clearly a pre-planned operation. Milosevic had specifically awakened the Serbs there to their position through the recalling of images of terror and persecution from the Second World War. The vicious media campaign was backed up by the stockpiling of weapons and supplies against war. As in Bosnia, Serbs were secretly armed by Belgrade, units of police were encouraged to defect, parallel radio communications were set up and the army was put in place to back up the Serbian irregular forces thus created.

Areas with significant Serb minorities in Krajina soon fell but many towns and cities almost on the border with Serbia were fiercely contested. The JNA, already shaken by its defeat at the hands of the Slovenes, found the Croatians, although initially poorly organised and equipped, to be tough and resilient fighters. JNA forces were also depleted by an estimated 50,000 men, Slovenian and Croatian soldiers having largely defected. In the east, Vukovar, on the Danube, was to take three months of shelling before it fell, and then all that remained for the Serbs were ruins. After the fall of Vukovar around November 19, the advance on the eastern front was halted. In military terms, it is hard to understand why an army of around 130,000 with access to some 1150 T54, T55A and M84 tanks (plus outdated models) should grind to a halt in the plains of Slavonija: perfect tank territory. The answer probably lies in the over extended front the army was now fighting on, combined with the unwillingness of the conscript foot soldier to fight. Without infantry back up the tank offensive could have been disastrous. Similarly, it is difficult to understand how the combined forces of the JNA and Chetniks failed to drive and hold a corridor north from Okucani through Lipik and Pakrac which would have enabled them to cut off the main supply route east around Virovitica denying food, munitions and other supplies to Osijek, Vukovar and Vinkovci. Eastern Slavonia could have been totally cut off with comparative ease in military terms.

Thus on the fronts in eastern and central Croatia and on the Dalmatian coast, the war settled into a long range artillery war with mortars, howitzers and rocket batteries subjecting the Croatian civil population to unpredictable and random attack. If the strategy was to demoralise the population and weaken the Croatian leadership it patently failed.

Meantime, the same sort of preparations for war were being made in Bosnia. Serbian elements in the interior ministry police force were encouraged to defect to a newly formed Serbian police force. Snipers were deployed in Sarajevo after the March 1 referendum bringing fear and instability to a degree far outwith their small numbers. Once the general political and social situation was destabilised - an operation which took only around three weeks - Serbian irregulars, again backed by the army, began to sieze territory in a strategy already tried and tested in Croatia.

The Bosnian Territorial forces - Croats and Muslims - were ill prepared, ill equipped and poorly organised. It is arguable that the Croats and Muslims would have been completely over run in the north of the country but for the direct intervention of the Croatian army from across the border. Men and equipment - 'volunteers' - flooded into the defence of beleagured towns like Bosanski Brod, Modrica and Tuzla, although by the end of July some towns had changed hands several times.

By the end of August 1992, the battle for Bosnia was virtually over on the ground. The country was effectively divided between Serb and Croat. The Serbs now held almost 70% of the country and the Muslims held little territory with the exception of Sarajevo and small pockets around the cities of Goradze and Bihac. Serbian tactics had effectively won the day in terms of *realpolitik* and Serbian leaders were able to present themselves at the London Conference on August 26 to negotiate from a position of considerable strength.

APPENDIX III

DRAMATIS PERSONAE

Adzic, General Blagoje Chief of Staff and acting defence minister until purged May 1992. Hardline Serb whose family was massacred by Croats during the Second War.

Izetbegovic, Alija President of Republic of Bosnia Herzegovina. Believed by many - particularly Serbs - to be dedicated to the establishment of a fundamentalist Islamic state in Bosnia.

Jansa, Janez Defence Minister, Republic of Slovenia. National hero after his arrest and imprisonment as editor of *Mladina* in 1988.

Kacin, Jelko Information Minister, Republic of Slovenia. Prominent as government spokesman during the Slovenian War.

Kadijevic, General Veljko Serbian defence minister until January 1992 (resigned after shooting down of EC helicopter).

Karadzic, Radovan Psychiatrist turned leader of Serbs in Bosnia. Widely believed to have instigated the conflict in BiH with the active support of Milosevic. Tough, uncompromising and contradictory in his public statements.

Kucan, Milan President, Republic of Slovenia.

Kukanjac, General Milutin Commander of Second Military District, including Bosnia, upon its independence. Relieved of command May 1992.

Macek, Brigadier Milan First chief of the Croatian Air Force (HRZ). Former Croatian pilot and instructor in Federal Air Force; defected to Zagreb on outbreak of war in Croatia.

Milosevic, Slobodan President, Republic of Serbia, from 1987. His personal political ambitions and desire to create a Greater Serbia are regarded by many as the fount of the conflicts throughout Yugoslavia. Described in May 1992 by the US Ambassador to Belgrade as "a con man and a liar".

Mladic, General Ratko Hardliner engaged in war in Croatia and in May 1992 appointed by self-styled Serbian Republic of Bosnia-Herzegovina to head JA forces in Bosnia.

Nambiar, Gen. Satis General commanding UNPROFOR forces in Croatia.

152

Panic, Milan Serbian American businessman appointed Prime Minister of Yugoslavia in July 1992. Regarded variously as a puppet of Milosevic, a plant and, almost universally, as something of an enigma, he quickly gained a reputation for promising what he was unable to deliver.

Panic, General Zivota Succeeded Adzic as Chief of Staff, May 1992

Paraga, Dobroslav Leader, Croatian Party of Rights (HSP).

Rupelj, Dimitrij Foreign Minister, Republic of Slovenia

Separovic, Zvonimir Foreign Minister, Republic of Croatia

Seselj, Vojislav Leader of the ultra-nationalist Serbian Radical Party

Tudjman, Franjo President, Republic of Croatia

Tus, General Anton Chief of Staff, Croatian armed forces.

APPENDIX IV
NOTES

1 Baptism of fire

The events described in this chapter took place during the course of fourteen visits to Slovenia, Croatia and Bosnia between June 1991 and May 1992. Extracts from this chapter appeared in *Frontline* in the *Sunday Mail Magazine* April 1992.

1 Edward Behr: *Anyone Here been Raped and Speaks English?* New York 1978

2 Quoted in *The Spectator*, July 1 1972

3 Mike Whitlam, Director General of the British Red Cross, in interview on the John Dunn Show, Radio Two, December 9 1991, 1830 hours

4 Quoted in *High Risk, Low Return* by Paul Jenks, *Daily Telegraph* page 15, September 25 1991

5 Peter Jenkins in *No new ways to halt this old slivovitz war, The Independent* page 19, November 12 1991

6 Phil Davison in *Battered Dubrovnik becomes second Beirut, The Independent* page 1, November 12 1991

7 Quoted in *A fate of bitterness and tears* by Anne McElvoy, *The Times* centre page, October 8 1991

8 Nenad Pejic interviewed by Ursula Ruston in *Index on Censorship*, June 1992

9 Evelyn Waugh: *Scoop*, London 1938

10 Michael Nicholson: *A Measure of Danger, Memoirs of a British War Correspondent*, London 1991

11 Don McCullin in interview with Danny Danziger in *The Independent* page 11, January 6 1992

12 Don McCullin: *Unreasonable Behaviour - An Autobiography,* London 1990

13 The Rt. Hon. Neville Chamberlain, Prime Minister, on BBC Radio September 28 1938, 2030 hours

14 P J O'Rourke: *Republican Party Reptile,* New York 1987

15 J Lucas: *Dateline Vietnam,* New York 1967

16 J A MacGahan in the *Daily News,* August 2 1876

17 Ed Vulliamy on *The Siege of Vukovar* in *The Guardian* October 21 1991

18 Martha Gellhorn: *The Face of War,* London 1959

19 Don McCullin: Interviewed by Terry Hope in *Amateur Photographer* April 11 1992.

20 John Le Carre: *The Honourable Schoolboy,* London 1977

21 Herbert Matthews: *The Education of a Correspondent,* New York 1946

22 Askold Krushelnycky: *Young Guns* in *The Sunday Times,* Style & Travel section, June 14 1992

2 On the sunny side of the Alps

The events in this chapter took place between Wednesday June 26 and Thursday July 4 1991. Extracts appeared in *Keeping a stiff upper lip in the war zone* in *Scotland on Sunday* July 7 1991.

1 John Steinbeck: *Once There was a War,* London 1959, from a dispatch for *The New York Herald Tribune*

2 Martha Gellhorn: *The Face of War,* London 1959, from a dispatch for *Collier's*

3 The highway to hell

The events in this chapter took place between September 28 and 30 1991. Extracts appeared in *Roadshow on highway to hell and back* in *Scotland on Sunday* October 6 1991.

1 P J O'Rourke: *Holidays in Hell*, New York 1988

2 Flavia Kingscote: *Balkan Exit*, London 1942

4 The bridge at Pokupsko

The events in this chapter at Pokupsko took place on Monday September 30 1991; those at Vidusevac on September 15. Extracts appeared in *Terror in the Croat killing fields* in *The Scotsman* October 4 1991 and in *An uphill struggle for the people's army* in *The Scotsman* September 19.

1 Martha Gellhorn: *The Face of War*, London 1959

2 Mehmet Husic quoted in *The Independent* June 18 1992

3 Ronnie Noble: *Shoot First*, London 1955

4 Martha Gellhorn, *ibid.*

5 Not so quiet on the Eastern front

The events in this chapter took place between October 25 and 27 1991; in December 1991 and in March 1992. Extracts appeared in *Shellshocked on the eastern front* in *Scotland on Sunday* November 3 1991 and the Dublin *Sunday Tribune* of the same date; and in *War respite for hostages of fortune* in the *Daily Express* January 21 1992.

1 Martha Gellhorn: *Shorty* in *The Honeyed Peace*, London 1954

6 The war on the innocents

The events in this chapter took place on Monday October 28. Extracts appeared in *Innocents at War* in *The Daily Express* November 5 1991; and *A war without winners* in *The Times Educational Supplement* October 11 1991.

1 Quoted in *War games that degrade the children of Yugoslavia* by Dusko Doder in *The European* page 10, November 22-4 1991

7 Killing the messenger

I interviewed Majda Glavasevic in Zagreb, December 26 1991. The translator was Danijela Nadj. Extracts from the interview appeared in *Where witnesses to war are silenced* in *Scotland on Sunday* January 5 1992.

8 Bosnian tinderbox

The events described at Bosanski Samac took place over the weekend of January 24 - 6 1992; those at Bosanski Brod over the weekends of February 29 - March 1 and April 18 - 20. Extracts appeared in *Divided Bosnia smoulders* in *Scotland on Sunday* February 2 1992; *Bosnia adds to dangers for UN forces* in *Scotland on Sunday* March 8 1992; *The first casualty at the outbreak of war* in *The Scotsman* April 24 1992; and *Divided by a river of despair* in *Scotland on Sunday* April 26 1992. Events at Modrica took place May 24-5 1992 and extracts appeared in *Summer madness down in Modrica* in *Scotland on Sunday* May 31.

9 Return from Vukovar

The events described took place between January 26 and January 28 1992. Extracts appeared in *A tortuous trip to the unknown* in *The Scotsman* February 1 1992.

10 All tanked up at the front

The events described took place in the third week of January 1992. Extracts appeared in *Private Snow White and a gran in a tank* in the *Daily Express* February 18 1992.

11 Don't they know it's Christmas?

The events at Djakavo took place on the Sunday of Christmas week, December 22 1991. The events at Karlovac December 24 - 5. A subsequent personal visit to the area around Sodolovci cast a certain amount of doubt on its location as the home village of the Croatian National Guardsmen who were killed, although this was the information given to the writer at the mortuary. It seems more likely that their home village was Semeljci and that they were on reconnaissance in the Sodolovci area, which was held by the Chetniks at that time.

Extracts appeared in *Christmas visits Croatia in a Jeep, Scotland on Sunday*, December 29 1991; and *Death laid bare, The Scotsman* December 31 1991.

12 Blue berets

Observation of Unprofor in Sector West and at Pleso took place during the last week of May 1992. Extracts appeared in *White knights in a deadly game of chess*, *The Scotsman* June 2 1992.

BIBLIOGRAPHY

Yugoslavia: History & Background

Glenny, Misha: *The Rebirth of History, Eastern Europe in the Age of Democracy*, London 1990
Trenchant political analysis by the BBC's Eastern European correspondent

Harrison, H D: *The Soul of Yugoslavia*, London 1941

Institute for War & Peace Reporting (eds.): *Breakdown: War & Reconstruction in Yugoslavia*, London 1992
Produced by Yugofax which has consistently endeavoured to present a balanced and impartial view of the conflict

Kingscote, Flavia: *Balkan Exit*, London 1942
Escape from Yugoslavia during the Second World War

McConville, Michael: *A Small War in the Balkans: British Military Involvement in Wartime Yugoslavia 1941 - 1945*, London 1986
Excellent military analysis which serves to highlight deficiencies in the military conduct of the present conflict

Maclean, Fitzroy: *Eastern Approaches*, London 1949
Political and military background to post-war Yugoslavia by Churchill's personal wartime envoy to Tito and the partisans

Maclean, Fitzroy: *Josip Broz Tito*, London 1980

Sirc, Ljubo: *Between Hitler and Tito*, London 1989
Best account of the post-war period available in English

West, Rebecca: *Black Lamb and Grey Falcon*, London 1942
The classic; a literary gem

Yovitchitch, Lena A: *Within Closed Frontiers*, London & Edinburgh 1956
Life in wartime Serbia

ABBREVIATIONS

BBC British Broadcasting Corporation (London, England)
BiH Bosnia Herzegovina
CSCE Conference on Security and Cooperation in Europe
CNN Cable News Network (based Atlanta, USA)
HDZ Croatian Democratic Union (ruling party)
HINA Croatian State News Agency
HOS Military wing of HSP
HRZ Croatian Air Force
HSP Croatian Party of Rights
HTV Croatian TV
HV Croatian Army
HVO Croatian Defence Council, Croatian Army in Bosnia
ICRC International Committee of the Red Cross
JA Yugoslav Army
JNA Yugoslav Federal Army
KOS Yugoslav counter-intelligence service
NATO North Atlantic Treaty Organisation
SDS Serbian Democratic Party, BiH
T55/72 Two most common types of tank in use
UNPROFOR United Nations Protection Force
UNHCR United Nations High Commissioner of Refugees
VBR Multiple rocket launcher
WEU Western European Union
WTN Worldwide Televsion News
ZNG Croatian Army formation, predecessor of HV

INDEX
of place names and people

Adams, Eddie 36
Adria Airways 50
Agence France Presse 53
Agotic, General 85, 95
Amini, Hassan 43-4
Argentina, Hotel (Dubrovnik) 21
'Arkan' 16
Arnett, Peter 25, 26
Auden, W H 41

Babena Greda 113, 114
Babic, Milan 16
Banja Luka 24, 104, 108
Barilovic 96
Baubic, General Bidac 17
BBC 24, 64, 101
Beaton, Cecil 44
Behr, Edward 13
Belgrade 60-1
Belgrade, Hotel (Sarajevo) 18
Bell, Martin 101
Bijeljina 16, 37, 110
Black Crows of Livanje, The 127-29
Blanchet, Pierre 20
Borba 28
Bosanski Brod 108-9, 110-12, 118
Bosanski Samac 103, 106
Bosna, Hotel (Banja Luka) 104
Bosna, Hotel (Sarajevo) 18, 31
Brcko 37, 114
Brnik Airport 21, 53-4
Bremner, Eric 24
Brest 74
Brysky, Peter 96
Bubalo, Alan 24

Capa, Robert 30, 35, 80
Carrington, Lord 78
Caythorpe, Lincs.43

Cepulic, Dr Mladen 93
Chamberlain, Neville 40
Chater, David 21
CNN 24, 36, 54, 56, 62
Crni Vrh 58

Daily Telegraph 22
Damon, Dan 31
Daruvar 141
Davison, Phil 21
Demirel, Suliman 105
Djakovo 41, 81, 124, 127, 130
Dobrinja 74
Domaljevac 113
Dosen, Mirjana 12
Dubica 40, 72-3
Dubrovnik 21, 36, 77, 102
Duga Resa 32-3, 97

Edinburgh Royal Infirmary 90
Edinburgh, Western General
    Infirmary 90
Ephron, Nora 45
Esplanade Hotel (Zagreb) 25, 60

Fattorini, Dr Ivan 90
Foca 105, 110

Gaddaffi, Colonel 105
Gaj 64
Gardovica, Nikolo 107
Gautier, Eric 136-37
Gellhorn, Martha 14, 56, 75, 83
Gill, Peter 13
Glavasevic, Bojan, Majda & Sinisa
    22, 98-101
Glas Slavonije 27
Guardian, The 27, 57
Gunja114-6
Gyori, Antoine 96

Hackett, Paul 40
Hammond, Graeme 139
Hadzic, Goran 16
Holiday Inn (Ljubljana) 55
Holiday Inn (Sarajevo) 18
Hollis, Phillip 22
Husic, Mehmet 74

Independent, The 29
Institute for Mothers & Children
  (Zagreb) 89-94
Intercontinental Hotel (Zagreb) 23,
  62, 125
ITN 69, 101
Ivan Dvor 86
Izbetbegovic, Alija 50

Jansa, Janez 57
Jenkins, Peter 20
Jenks, Paul 21-2, 43-4
Johnson, Senator Hiram 42
Johnson, Samuel 45

Kacin, Jelko 57
Kamenica 125-27
Karadzic, Radovan 106
Karlovac 12, 24, 29, 83, 97, 125,
  133-34
Klancej 123
Kloss, Stephan 97
Korac, Zarko 93
Korosec, Mateuz 56
Koruna, Hotel (Karlovac) 32
Kosovo 50
Kostajnica 24
Krajina 16
Krsticevic, Zivko 24, 29, 35, 95-8
Krushelnycky, Askold 44
Kumrovec 123
Kucan, President Milan 56, 57
Kupa, River 96
Kurenoi, Genady 22
Kutina 63

Le Carré, John 44
Life 36, 44
Lipica 86

Lipik
Lippizaner horses 41, 86
Ljubljana 52, 53
Lucas, Jim 42
Lynden, Aernout van 31

Mc Cullin, Don 37, 44
MacGahan, J A 43
Mariocenevic, Budimir & Ilija 86
Magyar Szo 28
Martin, Captain Douglas 142
Matthews, Herbert 44
Medvedjek 54
Mesic, Stipe 77
Middleton, Captain Ned 140
Mihaljevic, Mario 110
Milic, Goran 27
Milic, Dr Shelko 131, 132
Militic, Rozika 126-27
Mladina 57
Modrica 117-18
Montenegro
Morris, Chris 20
Moser, Bruno 97
Mostar 110
Most Mladosti 59
Murkovci 80

Nambiar, Gen. Satis 107
National Hotel (Belgrade) 60
New York magazine 45
Nogin, Victor 22
Nouvel Observateur 20
Nova Gradiska 81
Nustar 79, 80

Observer, The 40
Odzak 117, 118
Oganj rocket launcher 15, 72, 81
Orkan rocket launcher 15, 81
O'Rourke, P J 14, 63, 66
Osijek 17, 21, 26, 41, 60, 77, 89,
  95-6, 107, 128

Page, Tim 13
Pakrac 13, 38, 63, 66-8, 90
Paradzikovic, Snjezana 124

Paraga, Dobroslav 26
Pecnik 120
Pejic, Nenad 27
Petrinja 20, 74
Ploce 102
Podravska Slatina 85
Pokupsko 70-2, 75, 132
Prekopakrac 66, 68
Preseren, France 56
Price, Col. Christopher 138

Quemener, Olivier 24

Rashita, General Andrija 85, 95
Rawashdeh, Yasin 28
Raznjatovic, Zeljko ('Arkan') 16
Reuters 19, 55
Ricchiardi, Sherry 85
Rosenthal, Joe 30
Royal Canadian Regiment 140
Ruedin, Dominic 20
Rupelj, Dimitrij 57

Sachsiche Zeitung 97
Sarajevo 24, 31, 74, 107, 110
Sarajevo, TV 27, 35-6
Sava, River 108, 113
Scotland on Sunday 40
Semeljci 124
Sentilj 55
Seselj, Vojislav 28
Sirac 140
Sky News 31, 36
Slavonija, Hotel (Vinkovci) 26, 78
Slavonski Brod 111
Slavonski Samac 102, 106, 113, 121
Slobodna Dalmacija 27
Slon Hotel (Ljubljana) 55
Sodolovci 130
Soldier of Fortune 59
Stankovic, Ivan 24
Stanley, Henry Morton 39
Steinbeck, John 38, 55
Stock, Lauren v. der 21
Suhopolje 86-8
Suisse Romande, Radio 20

T-55 tank 15
Thermal Hotel (Daruvar) 144
Times, The 28
Tito, Josip Broz 123
Tito, Marshall Barracks (Zagreb) 97
Torbarina, Tanja 27
Trebnje 51
Trevisan, Dessa 28
Tudjman, President Franjo 27
Turanj 24, 35, 97, 134-37

UNPROFOR 104, 106-9, 138-42

Vasic, Milos 28
VBR rocket launcher 81
Vidusevac 70
Vinkovci 23, 26, 77, 78-9, 83, 90,
    91, 107, 130
Virovitica 86
Visnews 18
Visoka Greda 81
Vogel, Nick 21, 54
Vojvodina 50
Vremje 28
Vrhnika 52
Vukovar 17, 21, 22, 36, 77, 82, 89,
    98-101, 121, 128, 130
Vulliamy, Ed. 43

Werner, Norbert 21, 54
Wilson, Col. John 108
WTN (Worldwide Television News)
    18, 23-4, 95

Yutel 27

Zagreb 23, 24, 25, 29, 51, 59-60,
    121
Zagrebacki Blok (Vinkovci) 26
Zupanja 114
Zvornik 16, 102, 110

Belgrade students' view of the conflict between Serbs and Croats, June 1992.